Rich + Kath,
Thank[illegible]
friendshi[illegible]
guys!

Gold

FINDING THE GOD-GIVEN POTENTIAL IN EVERY LIFE

NICOLA NEAL

RIVER
PUBLISHING

River Publishing & Media Ltd
info@river-publishing.co.uk

www.river-publishing.co.uk

Cover image credit: Joel Mott

ISBN 978-1-908393-87-6

Printed in the UK by TJ International, Padstow, Cornwall

Contents

What Others Are Saying... 5

Acknowledgements 8

1. Mining for Gold 9
   - Nightmares and witchdoctors 9
   - Mining for Gold 16
   - Buried treasure 17

2. Accepted, Protected and Cared For 21
   - Stadiums and slums 21
   - What is your obsession? 23
   - Accepted, protected and cared for 25
   - Mama C 28

3. Love God, Love People, Love Yourself 35
   - Internal vs external 37
   - #blessed 38
   - Post it notes! 42
   - The power of agreement 44

4. The Small and Insignificant 47
   - Chickens, chickens, chickens 50
   - Mighty warrior 52
   - Take possession 54

5. Out of the Ashes 59
Perspectives 59
Death to life 62
Crisis 66
Here we go again 66
Beauty out of ashes 70

6. To the Ends of the Earth 73
Banda 75
Hidden beauty 79
Glorious grace and limitless love 80
Fashion accessories 82

7. Orphan-hood to Royalty 87
Gold carrier 87
In the presence of the King 90
Whitechapel 95

8. I See You 97
Ambassadors 102

9. The Simple Way 111
Moving home 115
God is good! 117
Yield 120
Storing up treasure 121
Stand up! 124

Our Story 127

What Others Are Saying...

"This is a powerful book for all those who want to grow more like Jesus. If we as the Church could see people as He sees them, and love them as He loves them, then the world would be changed!"
Paul Harcourt
National Leader, New Wine England

"Just as gold is processed and refined, this book has the potential to refine your heart and mould it for God's purposes. Nicola has written a personal but profound cry from the heart that is both hugely challenging and deeply compassionate. I am sure others will respond as I have – with a renewed commitment to others and a surrendered heart. I truly love this book and feel sure it will be a blessing to many."
Cathy Madavan
Speaker, Writer, Coach, and author of Digging for Diamonds

"Nicola firmly believes that every human being, regardless of earthly status, is a Gold-carrier. She lives this out from the slums of Uganda to the East End of London, and her stories of salvation and restoration are truly astounding. This is the stuff of the New Testament today and you will not fail to be undone by the beautiful truths of Jesus that she outlines, and the authentication of them in the lives of the poor and humble. This book is potentially life-changing for you and me. Nicola calls us to the wonder of finding and releasing the God-given Gold in ourselves and, in turn, in everyone else we meet. My heart leapt as I read this, my spirit was deeply stirred. This book is simply 'gold' as the title suggests!"
Anne Coles
New Wine

"What would life look like if we stripped everything away, yielded fully to Christ and chose the way of love? It might look like what you'll find in this book and the remarkable story of 'Every Life'. Be prepared to be moved and have your heart broken."
Carl Beech
Senior Leader, Redeemer King
Global President CVM

"In this challenging and encouraging read, Nicola reminds us that there is Gold everywhere, especially where we often least expect it. The question is, are we willing to pray, dig and fight to discover it? This book will open your eyes afresh to the good and gritty Gospel that is powerful enough to bring even witchdoctors to their knees."
Chris Sayburn
Head of Worship, New Wine England, Pioneer Curate - St Philips Chapel Street

"Nicola Neal has gifted us a timely book packed full of truth, wisdom, hope and courage. This book is both deeply challenging and hugely encouraging. Nicola and her team have first-hand experience of witnessing God find Gold in people living in some of the poorest and most difficult places on earth. Through a potent mix of theological reflection, profound stories and practical wisdom, we are invited to see that we too can partner with God to see every life redeemed, and be equipped to do it wherever He has placed us."
Rev Dr Rich Johnson
Vicar of All Saints Worcester & New Wine National Leadership Team

"As uncomfortable as it can be at times, we all need to face challenges that stretch us far beyond our comfort zones. Oftentimes, our greatest growth comes from giving ourselves to others, even those who are unable to give back. One of the most stretching invitations is when God calls us to see beyond the obvious and give ourselves to loving and serving people who may not yet see who they're called to be. But that is what God's people do: we see the value in each person. We often forget that the greatest of treasures can be found around dirt, but if we focus on the dirt, we will miss the treasure.

Nicola gives a great challenge to us in the Western Church about God's created treasure. She gives great insight into what it looks like to be a disciple, even in places where we wouldn't have believed God could use us. This book is challenging, at times uncomfortable, but a much-needed message for all of us."

Christy Wimber

Author, Pastor, Teacher, Church Planter

"Nicola tells stories and they are stories that shake hell to its core. This is Hope piercing the darkness. This is Love melting the hardness. This is the fragrance of Life that dispels the stench of death. Read this book and you'll be ruined for dull Christianity. Read it and shine like Gold!"

Rachel Gardner

Director at Youthscape, President Girls Brigade E&W, Founder of Romance Acadamy, Trustee – Home for Good

Acknowledgements

To my *Every Life* family around the world:

Thank you for so selflessly laying down your lives, each day on behalf of Jesus, to serve the poor. For not giving up when the going gets tough and for being prepared to sacrifice, sometimes greatly, to see so many find freedom. You are all my heroes in the faith, my daily inspiration, and you love so well.

To Simon, thank you for always seeing the GOLD in me, even when I have been unable to see it myself and for patiently, tirelessly and consistently mining for it. I am so grateful that I get to walk life by your side and I look forward to discovering more of what Jesus has in store for our family over the years to come. I love you.

To Tim Pettingale, I literally could not have done this without you! Thank you for seeing the "beauty in the chaos", for not giving up on me, and for so graciously and patiently helping me walk the process of creating this book. You have gone above and beyond and I am deeply grateful. We did it!

1. Mining for Gold

"There is God-given potential lying dormant within every person, just waiting to be released. In our ministry, we call it Gold."

Nightmares and witchdoctors

A few years ago, our Ugandan staff were reaching out to some of the men living in a nearby slum community. It involved spending time there at night, chatting with the locals in bars. Most of the men were recently out of prison and alcoholics or drug addicts. Most were caught up in the toxic mix of poverty and crime. Each Wednesday evening our team would hang out with them, get to know them better, and share about Jesus in between games of pool.

One evening as we were leaving the slum, we were approached by a young man who seemed desperate to talk. I will refer to him as "J".

J had lived in the slum for many years. For as long as he could remember, he had been having terrible nightmares. He described them as "night visitations". A dark presence would enter his home each evening and he would hear demonic voices telling him to do terrible things – both to himself and to others. He was terrified of the night and hadn't slept properly in years. He was exhausted, harassed and desperate.

J wasn't a Christian. He made it painstakingly clear that he didn't believe in Jesus himself, but he knew that our team did, and wondered if we would still be prepared to pray for him.

Of course, we were more than happy to pray. A group huddled around J in the dimly lit alleyway and prayed a very simple prayer.

A few weeks later a group of us were walking around that community when J appeared, clearly very excited. He had been looking for us and was excited to tell us what had happened to him.

"You won't believe what happened after you prayed!" was his opening line.

We smiled at one another, secretly thinking, *we probably can guess what happened!*

"Tell us," we said.

He went on to explain that since we had prayed for him, he'd not had a single nightmare or night-terror. There had been no more demonic visitations or demonic voices speaking to him.

"My fear of the dark has completely gone," he continued breathlessly, "and I've slept deeply each night. Better than I have in many years!"

He also explained how his home felt like a different place – full of peace and safety. We were thrilled!

J then asked if we would introduce him to the Jesus we had prayed to. Of course, we agreed, and J met Jesus that day, in an alleyway in the slum.

This was amazing, but the adventure was far from over…

A while later J asked if we would go and pray for his Auntie. He told us that she had been suffering in a similar way to him, so he wondered if Jesus might be able to help her as well.

J's Auntie didn't live in the slum, but in a town about 45 mins outside of Kampala. We arranged to go and visit her with him the following Saturday.

* * *

Saturday came and we set off in our car – me, another member of our leadership team and three interns we were currently training. We picked up J from the slum and headed for the town which was, allegedly, "About 45 minutes away..." We soon discovered we would have to travel much further than we first imagined.

As we entered the town, J told us to take a left and keep going, so we continued to drive. After another whole hour had passed, I was starting to feel quite concerned.

"Are we nearly there yet?" I asked J, sounding like a ten-year old.

"We are not going to the town," he explained, "but somewhere in the district."

The town and the district had the same name. However, this information was more than a little alarming, as the district covered a very large area. The realisation that this expedition was going to take a lot longer than I thought, and potentially be quite different to what I'd imagined, began to dawn on me. I asked J for more information about his Auntie.

"She is the Queen Witchdoctor of the region," he replied.

This meant that she was the highest-ranking witchdoctor for over 100 miles. People would travel vast distances to visit her and seek her power. She would have been dedicated to the demonic at birth and been used her whole life in ritual sacrifice. However, J told us that she had grown weary of witchcraft and its practice and wanted to break free from it.

She had bought herself a small plot of land just outside her village, where she planned to work the ground and grow vegetables to sell at the local market. This was her plan to earn an income for herself, so that she would no longer have to practise witchcraft for money.

Every time she tried to walk onto her land to dig, however, crossing the invisible village boundary line, she would instantly be paralysed from the neck down and be unable to move. The local villagers would come to pick her up and carry her back to her shrine, where she would recover and continue to practise her witchcraft, in order to have enough money to buy food to eat.

I was stunned by this information! This was not what I thought we'd signed up for. To say I was a little overwhelmed by the situation would be putting it mildly.

After almost three hours of driving along the dusty, potholed roads of the bush, we turned onto a narrow dirt track. J announced that we should now pull over, as we would have to travel the rest of the way on foot.

At this point, I began to get quite nervous. I had gone along with the whole story until now, but in reality, I knew nothing about J. We had had two very brief interactions with him, and now we were miles from anywhere with no mobile phone signal. Plus, we were about to follow him, on foot, deeper into the African bush!

My heart began to beat fast as he led us deeper into the overgrowth. I had one eye on the ground to make sure we didn't stand on any snakes and the other on J, following his lead. All the time I was frantically praying and asking Jesus to HELP!

Various scenarios ran around my mind. What kind of situation were we about to walk into? Images ranging from an Elijah-type showdown with the prophets of Baal, to all of our decapitated heads on poles arranged around the village flashed through my mind. Yes, I was scared!

A short while later we emerged from the bush into a small clearing, and before us was a beautiful little village of mud huts with grass roofs. There was a clearing in the middle and people were dotted around, busily preparing food, cooking and sweeping.

Taking in the surroundings, I spotted a grey-haired old lady in the distance. She was small in stature, but something about her grabbed my attention. She was looking the other way, but as soon as she turned and caught sight of us, she began to shout and jump up and down. Then she ran across the clearing and threw herself at our feet. She was shouting something over and over, but I couldn't make out what it was.

"Is this your Auntie?" I asked J. "What is she saying?"

"She is saying, 'Give me Jesus, give me Jesus, give me Jesus!" he said.

For a few moments I felt like I was in a dream. It all seemed too easy and nothing made sense. We helped the lady to her feet and one of our team began to explain the Gospel to her. She was told who Jesus was and what it would mean for her life if she chose to follow Him. In fact, we went to great lengths to make sure she *really* understood the consequences: the changes it would demand; the implications for her life; the personal cost to her if she decided, that day, to submit her life to Jesus.

In the West, at times we have been guilty of selling a cheap Gospel – a watered-down, sanitised version of what it really means to be a disciple of Jesus. We were determined not to do that today – especially not with this lady. She needed to be fully aware of what she was signing up for. It was certainly going to be life changing for her. It may literally cost her life.

After painstakingly laying it all out for her as clearly as we could, she was still asking to meet with Him, so we had the great joy of introducing her to Jesus that afternoon. It was a beautiful moment.

We then suggested, in order to remove the temptation to return to her former lifestyle of witchcraft, that we should burn all of her witchcraft and sorcery paraphernalia. She thought this was a great idea and began to pile it all up outside her shrine. Then she promptly set it on fire. We all stood there, staring at the fire as it blazed, slightly stunned by the events that had unfolded. Then one of our interns asked,

"What should we do now?"

In truth, I didn't really know! But it seemed that maybe we should just worship and glorify Jesus – so that's what we did. The memory of us singing and dancing around the fire with this lady is etched into my mind forever. It was such a precious, mind-blowing, powerful and humbling moment to be a part of.

As you can imagine, the events of that afternoon drew plenty of attention, and later we shared the Gospel with the whole village. In response, men, women and children – everyone, in fact, apart from one person – gave their lives to Jesus.

We wondered whether we would ever be able to find this remote village again, so we decided to baptise each person there and then, using the one jerry can of water we'd brought with us. Then we prayed for them all to be filled with the Holy Spirit.

It was the most surreal and wonderful afternoon of my life! I am so thankful that I was able to capture on my phone a short clip of us baptising the former witchdoctor, and of her dancing and worshipping just a few moments later.

We left late that afternoon, still marvelling at all we had seen Jesus do. On the long drive home, I replayed the day's events in my mind. It had been the kind of supernatural outpouring that I'd only ever read about in books. I never imagined I'd have the honour of witnessing, or being a part of, something like this myself.

A few weeks later we did find the village again and I checked in on this lady to see how she was doing. I knew that not only would this event have a huge impact on her, but the news of it would travel far and wide. I wanted to see how she was coping and to give her a Bible.

That afternoon as we sat together, sharing a plate of freshly roasted ground nuts and sipping chia, I asked her the question that had been burning in my heart.

"Why, on that day, did you immediately decide to follow Jesus?"

Her response stunned me, so I immediately wrote it down, so I wouldn't forget it:

"The moment you walked into my village, I realised that the power inside of you was far greater than the power that was inside of me, and I knew I had to bow the knee to it."

Beautiful.

Mining for Gold

When we walked in that community, we had no clue what we were letting ourselves in for! We didn't have a "witchdoctor salvation strategy" or indeed any kind of plan. We had no past experience to draw on. We had no one to advise us what to do. We had nothing in our hands and no clever words on our lips. We were both unprepared and untrained for the task at hand. All we had was a reliance on Jesus to help us, come what may.

It has always been my belief that our role as leaders is to make ourselves redundant as soon as possible. The point of leadership is to raise up those who are coming behind us and see them released into the fullness of their God-given potential. For that reason, I have always made sure that it is our team members who get to "do the stuff", while I have the joy of standing on the side-line giving instructions and cheering them on.

The same was true this day. I was keen that our interns should play as big a role as possible, so we encouraged them to be the ones who prayed, helped lead the villagers to Jesus, baptised them and prayed for them to be filled with the Holy Spirit.

It was a deeply rewarding and joyful experience for me to see them shine in this way, and to experience for themselves the power and presence of God working through them!

A few hours later, however, I discovered something that literally blew my mind.

As the team chatted during the car journey home, we discovered that one of our interns was not actually a believer. In fact, he was an active Muslim! Two things immediately occurred to me:

First, how on earth had we not picked up this little fact during our recruitment process? I must have a word with our head of HR!

Second, the revelation hit me that Jesus is so completely and totally outside of any box I've ever tried to put Him in. His ways are really NOT ours! If He wants to, He can use anyone, even the most unqualified person, to do whatever He wants done. He can even use a young Muslim man to lead a Queen ranking witchdoctor to Jesus! Amazing!

Buried treasure

I believe that there is God-given potential lying dormant inside every person, just waiting to be released. In our ministry, we call it *Gold*.

It doesn't matter whether you were born in the West or in the developing world. Whether you grew up amongst the most affluent, or amongst the world's poor. Where you come from is irrelevant – that's just geography. What matters is who created you and what treasure He invested in you when He did so.

I believe that the words of Psalm 139 are true for everyone:

For you created my inmost being;
you knit me together in my mother's womb.
I praise you because I am fearfully and wonderfully made;
your works are wonderful,
I know that full well.
My frame was not hidden from you
when I was made in the secret place,
when I was woven together in the depths of the earth.
Your eyes saw my unformed body;
all the days ordained for me were written in your book
before one of them came to be.
(Psalm 139:13)

Father God formed you, He created you, He purposed you, He destined you.

The reality of *who you are*, and the potential of your life, is not based on your natural circumstances. It has nothing to do with your past or your present. What the people around you or society has to say about you has no bearing on it. *Who you are* is based only on who your supernatural Creator is, and what HE says is true about you. He sees the Gold. He put it there.

Sometimes that Gold, that God-given potential, gets buried under the dirt of life. It is suffocated by poverty, religion, pain and adverse circumstances. As believers, my job and yours is to walk alongside others and help to mine for that Gold in them; to uncover the buried treasure. We are called to see individuals, families, and whole communities released into the fullness of their God-given destiny and potential; to walk in the fullness of life that Jesus talks about:

> *The thief comes only to steal and kill and destroy, I have come that they may have life and have it to the full.* (John 10:10)

The fundamental calling on each of our lives is this: simply, to go and make disciples. This means much more than securing a person's eternal destiny. It's about…

…empowering others to live their lives in the way Jesus demonstrated.

…helping them to fulfil their God-given purpose and calling, wherever and whatever that looks like.

...the call to love Him, then help to draw others deeper into His love.

...knowing Him and making Him known.

...following Him, then teaching others to do the same.

...first learning how to mine for Gold in our own lives, then in the lives of our families, our neighbours, our community and our nation.

It is my deep conviction that no life is too messy, no heart too broken, no situation too dark for the love of Jesus to come in, transform it, and make something beautiful from it – just like He did in the village that day.

The "mess" of life can be scary to our Western mind and culture. We do everything we can to avoid it, to distance ourselves, to try to contain it. I dare to suggest that we are called to do the exact opposite! We must identify the darkest, most broken, messiest, chaotic places that exist in this world and purposefully walk right into the centre of them, to see the transforming power and love of Jesus break in and form something beautiful out if it all.

Our challenge and adventure is to see beyond all the chaos, to identify the God-given Gold and boldly and courageously begin the process of mining it.

Is it risky? Of course.

Jesus never promised that the life He has called us to would be easy, uncomplicated and risk free. In fact, He clearly stated the opposite

In this world you will have trouble. (John 16:33)

However, He also made a very clear promise to us in the same breath:

But take heart! I have overcome the world.

God has a plan and a purpose for each life. There is always hope, always love, always grace readily available for anyone who wants to partake of it.

There is always restoration, always redemption waiting to wrap itself around every heart and situation.

There is always beauty to be found, destiny to be recovered, Gold to be discovered. Will we be the ones who mine for it?

2. Accepted, Protected and Cared For

"He is not put off by your mess and your brokenness.
Instead, right there in the place of your deepest shame,
insecurity and vulnerability, He calls you by name.
He takes you by the hand and begins to walk WITH
you into your freedom and destiny."

Stadiums and slums

It had been one of those intense days. You know, the sort where you are processing so many things in your mind that by the end of it, you are exhausted and just need to switch off and unwind. I'd had a particularly difficult and extremely hot day in the slum communities. I arrived home depleted in every way.

Before I immersed myself in the busyness of making dinner for my family, I turned on my computer and sat down to watch a short worship video that I love. It usually takes me into that place of inner rest and stillness, ready to unwind with Jesus.

I'm not sure how it happened, but the video I was expecting to play didn't. Instead, a 15-minute clip of a conference began. I wasn't even aware that I had this on my computer. It was simply titled "Spontaneous Worship" and, as I watched, I was undone.

Let me explain:

The clip shows around 15,000 men and women, lost in spontaneous song to the Lord. It was beautiful, moving and profoundly impacting. I watched, transfixed, as wave after wave of spontaneous worship erupted around the stadium until the whole place was exploding with dance and song.

As I watched, I wept and all I could whisper to the Lord was, "This is what you deserve."

He is so worthy. He is so very deserving of our worship; of our continual love and adoration; of endless voices lifted high in exaltation; the sound of the masses raised in ceaseless song, declaring and proclaiming His magnificent splendour and glory.

If the whole earth joined together right now – every single nation, every tribe, every tongue – and worshipped Him ceaselessly until the end of days, it still would not be enough to express just how very worthy and utterly deserving He is.

As I watched this little video – 15 minutes, 15,000 people – what blew my mind all over again was this:

This all-powerful God, who created the heavens and the earth, who breathed stars into existence and spoke light into being; who formed man from the dust and breathed life into him. This God, who holds the universe in His hands, who is all-consuming light and fire; this God who dwells in the praise of cathedrals and stadiums; this all-powerful, all-knowing, beautiful, holy, righteous God… He chooses to come and hang out with us each day in the filth, dirt and the stench of the slum.

Here is the truth:

He is not confined to a building.

He is not concerned with His surroundings.

He is not drawn by the beauty of ancient architecture or the magnificence of man-made structures.

Neither is He repulsed by the stench of raw, free-flowing sewage, or disease-filled alleyways and passageways.

Instead, He is consumed with a love for the hearts of the people He finds in all of those places. He chooses to manifest Himself right there with them, wherever they may be.

He DESERVES stadiums, but He CHOOSES slums!

What is your obsession?

During the days that followed this experience, the Lord began to speak to my heart in a way that was both captivating and deeply uncomfortable. He began to challenge the very foundations that I had, until this point, built much of my belief on.

He began one day by simply saying,

"Nicola, our obsession is not the same … you seek perfection, but I seek hearts. You chase the beautiful, I chase the broken. You pursue excellence, I pursue the lost. You want the best, I desire the most despised."

As I said, deeply uncomfortable!

It's interesting to me how we all seem to be searching for some idealistic form of perfection. We are always looking to upgrade our lives: to have the nicer car, the bigger house, the ever-expanding wardrobe, the more impressive education. We have bought into the deception that these things will somehow give us greater credibility – not just with others, but even with ourselves. We think that these things will justify our existence and prove our worth.

We are so easily seduced by the attraction of outer Gold, rather than inner Gold. We accept the lie that destiny and fulfilment are found in material possessions and man-appointed positions. We easily convince ourselves that we are defined by how the world sees us, not by who God says we are. Then we wonder why we are constantly insecure and live in fear of failure.

The problem with this approach to life is that its flaws quickly become apparent – even to us. We hide our true selves from view, cover up our inadequacies with material possessions and accolades, and desperately hope that people won't look any deeper into our lives than what can be seen on the surface. We fear that if they do, they will realise that we are, in fact, a fraud, living a masquerade. If others dig deep enough, they might discover who we really are and uncover our weakness, brokenness, fear and pain.

From our church pulpits we preach that we are all wonderfully loved; that we can rest secure in that love and acceptance. We are desperate to avoid admitting that, in reality, this has rarely been our experience. We are haunted by the thought that if the members of our congregation knew who we *really were*, they would turn their backs on us in contempt.

The antidote to this paradox is to fill our lives with endless busyness. We bury our real selves under a camouflage of good deeds and spirituality, presenting to the world a version of ourselves we believe to be pleasing and acceptable. Sadly, by default, we are giving power to the very thing that is crushing and ultimately destroying us. We quietly die inside through the loneliness and pain of not being *truly known*.

To be known is what we truly crave. Deep down it's all we long for. Not more accomplishments, but acceptance. Not more possession, but to be truly seen; to be accepted and loved.

How do our church communities fare on this issue?

In the place where the sinner, the broken, the least and the lost should always find a home, and where grace should abound and love be all-consuming, do we instead find religion and judgement? A set of standards we all fear we will never reach? Yet, we persist in projecting such standards onto one another, each of us scrambling to attain them.

As believers we are often our own worst critics. We are good at putting ourselves down and constantly play the game of comparison. We compare our bodies, our marriages, our children, work life, social life, spiritual life, and the list goes on. We seem to decide so easily that we fail on so many levels. We are not godly enough, kind enough or holy enough to truly be *acceptable* to God. Or we are not gifted enough, educated enough, or anointed enough to be *used* by Him.

In one fell swoop we disqualify ourselves from both His love and His service.

How can we see another perspective?

Let me respond with two stories: one from the Bible and the other of a lady I met.

Accepted, protected and cared for

Here, I believe, is the heart of our problem: how we see ourselves is often in opposition to how God sees us.

What we say about ourselves (or what others say about us that we accept and believe) is often contrary to what God says about us.

Understanding the truth of how God feels about us, and what He says about us, will therefore radically alter our perspective.

Mark chapter five tells the well-known story of the woman who had an on-going blood-related illness. In the primitive society in which Jesus lived, women were considered to be little more than property and were often labelled as evil, ignorant and immoral. They were not allowed to enter certain parts of the temple and were segregated from the men in the synagogues. Women were considered inferior to even servants. They were not allowed to talk to men in public and were not permitted to testify in a court of law, since women were considered unreliable witnesses.

In this account we see a woman – already disadvantaged, taking into account all of the above – who has been bleeding for 12 years. This was very bad news for her. At this time, a woman who was menstruating was considered to be "ceremonially unclean" for seven days. Anything she touched was rendered unclean and all sorts of cleansing rituals had to be performed to restore "order". This lady, however, had been bleeding constantly for years.

According to the purity laws of the Old Testament, a person with an issue of blood was, in effect, permanently quarantined. She would have been shunned by her community, even her own family. A woman with this problem was simply not welcome in society.

Mark tells us that this woman had spent everything she had trying to get better. She had sought every possible medical cure and consulted the best doctors available, but nothing had worked. It seemed that she was incurable. Luke also gives account of this story and adds that, despite everything, she had "just grown worse".

One day, likely from the periphery of the crowd, she spotted Jesus walking along. In her utter desperation, she pushed through the throng of people surrounding Him and managed to grab the hem of His cloak. Immediately, Jesus felt power leave Him, so He stopped to ask those around Him,

"Who touched me?"

I often wonder how this lady felt in that moment, as Jesus spoke those words. Culture said that she was an outcast – unacceptable, unclean, unworthy – certainly not allowed to touch a man, let alone a Rabbi, let alone Jesus! I imagine she must have braced herself for a rebuke and further rejection as she took a deep breath and, in fear and trembling, replied,

"I did."

Jesus' response to her is nothing short of breath taking. Reading this event through the filter of the modern Western mind set, where women are valued as equal members of society, it's hard to grasp the full impact of what Jesus did and said. As she stands before Him in her uncleanliness, despised and rejected by society, waiting for yet more scorn, Jesus looks at her and says simply,

"Daughter…"

The root of the word translated here as "daughter" means "accepted, protected and cared-for".

What an amazingly outrageous, culturally unacceptable, wonderfully politically-incorrect statement! As well as healing her, with a single beautiful word, Jesus wiped away all of the rejection and shame this woman had suffered.

He speaks the same thing over you and me today:

"Accepted, protected, cared for."

The truth is, no matter what you feel about yourself, what others have said about you, or what you have or haven't done with your life – you are accepted, protected and cared for by God.

Regardless of the situations you've found yourself in, and the bad decisions you've made over the years – you are accepted, protected and cared for by God.

No matter how much of a failure you feel, and how eaten up you are with shame and guilt – you are accepted, protected and cared for by God.

However unclean you feel, or however unacceptable you think you are – He calls you accepted, protected and cared for!

Mama C

I have a friend who lives in a slum. I will call her Mama C.

Mama C was desperate, poor and caught up in a life of prostitution. Each day she would sell her body in order to have enough money to feed her daughter and support her addictive lifestyle.

The first day I met her, I fell in love.

She was one of the funniest, most vibrant people I had ever met and, to the best of her ability, she lived out her life with as much dignity as she could. I would visit her as often as I could and sit with her on the little step outside her house.

Regardless of how filthy she was, how drunk or high, I would hold her in my arms and tell her she was precious; that she was loved, by me and most importantly by Jesus.

I was never invited into her home and often there were strange men waiting for her inside or standing outside, ready to pay for her services. Sometimes I could see she had marks on her face and arms where she had been beaten and thrown to the floor.

One day when I met with her, her injuries were far more serious than I had ever seen before. Her face was swollen almost beyond recognition. Her body was covered in bruises and wounds and she had burn marks around her neck where someone had tried to strangle her.

She had reported what had happened to the police, but they had heard she was a prostitute, so turned her away and refused to help. They said that since she was a prostitute, she deserved everything she got. The local community leaders were not helpful either and, sadly, neither was the church. Both said the same as the police.

Meanwhile, Mama C was broken, bruised and terrified. We sat together in the dirt, unsure what to do next. I didn't know how best to help her, but we began to talk about Jesus. We told her about His love for her, about how He called her "daughter" and how she was accepted, protected and cared for by Him.

We prayed for her and continued to speak about Jesus' love for her, and it felt as though she was soaking in every word. On that Wednesday afternoon, sat in the dirt of the slum, filthy, beaten and broken, Mama C gave her life over to Him.

Seeing her encounter Jesus for the first time was nothing short of breath taking. What a privilege it was to witness Him coming and manifesting Himself to her, right there in the midst of her deep shame and brokenness. We watched her face light up as His presence began to surround her. The fear, trauma and pain that had been written so clearly in her eyes, etched into her face, slowly began to fade. In its place, a radiant light and joy began to appear. It was a very precious, beautiful moment that I will never forget.

I would love to be able to tell you that after that day, Mama C never drank again, never took drugs and left her lifestyle of prostitution behind. But I can't.

She still drank, still took drugs, and still sold her body sometimes in order to feed her family. Did that frustrate me? Of course it did! I was desperate for her to break out of that lifestyle and experience complete freedom from it. One afternoon, when my frustration felt all-consuming, the Lord spoke to me very clearly.

"Nicola, your job is not to get frustrated. Instead, it is to love – to love her out of the arms of men and in to the arms of my Son, Jesus."

So that is what our team gave itself to do.

We would visit her as often as we possibly could, pray with her, read the Bible together, call out the Gold we knew was in her, and talk about the "hope and future" Father God had destined for her.

The days I was able to go and visit her were always my favourite. She would sit with me on the dirt step outside her home, often wrapped in nothing more than a sheet, with a customer waiting for her inside her little one-room house. She would lay her head in my lap and say,

"Pray for me."

So, I did.

We would pray and worship together, then I would read her something from the small Bible I always kept in my back pocket. God's presence would come so tangibly at times, that it would utterly overwhelm us both.

Over years I have had the joy of visiting some of the most famous centres of revival in the world. I have knelt on the carpets of some of the world's most anointed places and stood amidst the grandeur of the most spectacular cathedrals. But I can honestly say, I have not experienced God's presence in those places as deeply as I have on the step outside Mama C's house, in the heat and dirt of the slum.

The truth is that Jesus finds Mama C irresistible! He is consumed with love for her. His love is always reaching out to her, even in the darkest, most sin-filled moments of her life.

Does He want her to stay trapped in her lifestyle?

No. But still He comes.

He meets her exactly where she is, right there in the place of her deepest shame, sin and brokenness. Then, He takes her by the hand and walks with her into freedom.

All Mama C had ever known was rejection from those in authority and hatred from her family. The men she had known had abused her and used her body for their own pleasure. Others turned and looked the other way when she was beaten, saying that she deserved the violence she suffered. Church pastors had told her that in order for her to be acceptable to Jesus, she first had to clean herself up, stop drinking, stop smoking, put on a nice a dress and attend a Sunday morning meeting!

Religion had told her to sort herself out in order to approach Jesus. But Jesus was stood in front of her with His arms wide open saying,

"Mama C, come just as you are. I will make you whole. I will make you clean, because I call you daughter – accepted, protected and cared for."

On another afternoon on Mama C's doorstep, we were chatting and laughing while her daughter played a few feet away and a stranger was waiting for her in her bed. In the midst of our laughter and conversation, Jesus spoke to me clearly, saying,

"Nicola, you and Mama C, you are the same..."

That got my attention. I was shocked!

"Err, what do you mean, Jesus?" I asked. This was His response:

"Mama C may be a prostitute living in a slum, and you may be a missionary living in a nice little house down the road, but your hearts are the same. You are asking the same questions: 'Am I loved? Am I acceptable?'"

Of course, He was right!

All of us ask those same questions, at one level or another, on a daily basis. One of the enemy's most powerful tactics is to convince us that we are too broken to be accepted. That we have made too many mistakes. That we are too weak and our lives too messy for us to be loved by God and used for His kingdom purposes. This is a lie that we must break agreement with. The truth is simple, and it is this:

> YOU ARE LOVED, YOU ARE ACCEPTED, YOU ARE PROTECTED, AND YOU ARE CARED FOR.

Just like the woman in Mark chapter 5 and my friend Mama C, Jesus stands in front of you today with a smile on His face, love in His heart, and His arms open wide. He is calling you to come to Him, JUST AS YOU ARE!

He is not put off by your mess and your brokenness. Instead, in the place of your deepest shame, insecurity and vulnerability, He calls you by name. He takes you by the hand and begins to walk WITH you into your freedom and destiny.

Throughout the last 10 years of working in very poor and often deeply broken and chaotic communities, we have made friends with some of the world's most rejected and despised – prostitutes, addicts, criminals and more. Time and again I have seen the love of Jesus manifest itself right there, in the midst of brokenness, without restriction or restraint. Through it all I have come to discover that His love and grace is always reaching out. It is constantly available, to anyone who wants to receive it – even those trapped in the most sin-filled, dark places.

His love is not conditional, nor is it selective for a chosen few. Instead is relentless, inexhaustible and unending.

His love is vast. It is deep, it is wide, and it is high (Ephesians 3:18).

Although you can easily discount yourself from being worthy to receive it, He does not discount you. Instead, He counts you! He counts you as precious. He counts you as His treasure. Even with all your imperfections and vulnerabilities, He calls you lovely. And it is there, in the midst of your weakness, that His power is made utterly *perfect*.

> *"But he said to me, 'My grace is sufficient for you, for my power is made perfect in weakness.'"* (2 Corinthians 12:9)

He is calling you today, to come just as you are. Go to Him now, and He will wrap His arms around you and begin to form you in His image. Allow Jesus to uncover the Gold He has placed within you. Then, you can go hunting for Gold in others.

3. Love God, Love People, Love Yourself

"How we see ourselves, and how well we learn to love ourselves, will have a direct impact on our ability to see and love others … Unless we recognise the Gold that we carry, we will never be able to uncover it in others."

In the previous chapter I wrote about the disconnect between how we see ourselves and how God sees us. In this chapter I want us to continue to dig into this theme of *identity*.

Why is this so important?

How you see yourself will have a profound impact on your life and how you live it out. Ultimately, your self-image doesn't just affect you. How you see yourself affects how you see others. More importantly, how you learn to *love yourself*, will have a direct impact on your ability to love others. Let me explain…

We are probably all familiar with the verse in Luke 10:27 where, in response to a question from an expert in religious law about "the most important commandment", Jesus responds:

"You must love the Lord your God with all your heart, all your soul, all your strength, and all your mind…"

It is one of Jesus' most well-known statements in all of Scripture. He continues, saying,

"And, 'Love your neighbour as yourself.'"

I find this second part fascinating. In the Church it is very popular to distil these two clear commands (known as the Great Commandment and the Great Commission) into one phrase:

"Love God and love people".

However, in our desire to simplify Jesus' command, to make it easier to understand and apply to our lives, we have lost a vital part of the picture. We have truncated Jesus' words and eliminated "as yourself".

Jesus points out that you need to love others *as yourself.* What happens then if, in fact, we love ourselves deficiently?

The truth is, in order to love others well, we first need to learn to love ourselves. We can only truly love others from a place of personal wholeness. So often we neglect ourselves, or at best have a dysfunctional self-image, and don't realise that we are sabotaging our best efforts to love others. If we don't really love ourselves, loving others isn't just hard – it's impossible.

It's not often that you'll hear a preacher speaking on the importance of loving yourself. If you are anything like me, you might dismiss such a message as a bit shallow and biblically weak. It might come across as a self-centred, over-spiritualised self-help message, with the odd word of Jesus thrown in for good measure. Personally, I don't have much time for that.

Yet, if the scripture above is true (and, of course, it is) then we need to grapple with what it really means to love ourselves and, equally, what it *doesn't mean.*

What does loving ourselves look like today, in our self-obsessed, hyper-self-aware social media culture?

Internal vs external

The world tries hard to convince us that in order to love yourself, you need to do one or more of the following:

- Indulge your wants and desires
- Be a little bit selfish (after all, *you're worth it*)
- Spend what you don't have
- Buy that nicer car, bigger house, designer clothing and accessories
- Etc, etc…

Our culture is heavily invested in the lie that in order to make your heart feel better, to feel happy and loved, you need to perfect your outer world. Once you do that, then your inner needs will be met.

It's amazing how easy it is to legitimise all of the above until they become "necessities" in life. We convince ourselves that we shouldn't have to – indeed *cannot* – live without them. We think that filling our world with this *external gold*, will somehow result in the validation and acceptance we desire.

It's also amazing what strategies for life we will implement in the belief that they will lead to inner peace:

We do all we can to relieve any stress or strain we're experiencing, seeking a life of comfort and ease.

We try to eliminate risk and avoid conflict.

We fall in line with celebrity culture and focus on our external appearance, in the belief that if everything looks beautiful on the outside, everything will be well on the inside.

We use the biblical call to a life of *rest* as an excuse for spiritual laziness, twisting this truth to suit our own purposes – deciding that sacrifice and offerings are not really what the Lord requires of us; that He is more interested in our contrite hearts. Thus, we circumvent the need for any real cost to our Christian lives.

We pick and choose from Scripture on a selective basis. We can all quote the verses that promise us "life in abundance" and speak of the amazing things God has in store "for those who love Him" but forget the part about "taking up our cross daily". As such we model to the world a form of Christianity that isn't much different to the life they are already living.

I think Christians today have been subtly sucked into the culture of entitlement that exists in society. We pray for parking spaces and airplane upgrades and count it as spiritual success when those prayers are answered. We post our wining pictures all over the internet declaring that we are *#blessed*.

I understand the thinking behind these things, but I find it a questionable (and possibly misleading) interpretation of what having God's blessing really means.

Let's consider for a moment how Jesus describes what *#blessed* looks like.

#blessed

When Jesus saw his ministry drawing huge crowds, he climbed a hillside. Those who were apprenticed to him, the committed, climbed with him. Arriving at a quiet place, he sat down and taught his climbing companions. This is what he said:

"You're blessed when you're at the end of your rope. With less of you there is more of God and his rule.

"You're blessed when you feel you've lost what is most dear to you. Only then can you be embraced by the One most dear to you.

"You're blessed when you're content with just who you are—no more, no less. That's the moment you find yourselves proud owners of everything that can't be bought.

"You're blessed when you've worked up a good appetite for God. He's food and drink in the best meal you'll ever eat.

"You're blessed when you care. At the moment of being 'care-full,' you find yourselves cared for.

"You're blessed when you get your inside world—your mind and heart—put right. Then you can see God in the outside world.

"You're blessed when you can show people how to cooperate instead of compete or fight. That's when you discover who you really are, and your place in God's family.

"You're blessed when your commitment to God provokes persecution. The persecution drives you even deeper into God's kingdom.

"Not only that—count yourselves blessed every time people put you down or throw you out or speak lies about you to discredit me. What it means is that the truth is too close for comfort and they are uncomfortable. You can be glad when that happens—give a cheer, even!—for though they don't like it, I do! And all heaven applauds. And know that you are in good company. My prophets and witnesses have always gotten into this kind of trouble."

(Mathew 5:1–12 MSG)

And not an airplane upgrade in sight!

Don't get me wrong: I know that Father God cares deeply about every aspect of our lives. I don't have an issue with praying for a car parking space, or even a more comfortable flight, as long as these things are not *all* I'm seeking after. It's essential that receiving such things does not become the sole definition of me being blessed and spiritually successful.

Personally, I am deeply challenged when I read Philippians 4:11:

> *For I have learned to be content whatever the circumstances. I know what it is to be in need, and I know what it is to have plenty. I have learned the secret of being content in any and every situation, whether well fed or hungry, whether living in plenty or in want. I can do all this through him who gives me strength.*

Having possessions is not wrong. Enjoying physical rest, entertainment, and doing things for ourselves is not bad. Our Father cares more about what we need to make our lives complete than we do, because He understands us far better than we understand ourselves. He is a good Father who enjoys giving His children gifts for no good reason. He delights in pouring out His abundance on us.

Yet, such unwarranted blessing is not a sign of our spiritual success, just of His grace. Whether we are blessed with possessions, wealth and success, or not, we need to learn Paul's lesson: to hold onto these things lightly. We must ensure that we are consumed with the pursuit of God, rather than fashion, fortune or fame. We must pursue the One who is truly worthy of glory and make Him the deepest longing of our hearts.

Everyone is searching to find a sense of inner peace, but that peace can only be found in one place. It is critical that we learn to nurture an inward thankfulness and gratefulness for God's grace, because the blessing that Jesus describes stems from this place of thankfulness. The issue of our self-identity and security can only be settled in God's love for us, which knows no bounds and no restrictions. We will know who we really are when we are fully rooted, grounded and established in Him and His love for us.

Anything else will always fall short.

Any man-made strategy for building self-worth will inevitably fail at some point. Jesus is the only one who is relentlessly consistent in His passionate pursuit and love for you. He is the only one who will never let you down, never cause you to question who you are, and never leave you to wonder if you are wanted.

Do you want to know true peace and joy?

Then you have to discover more of Him.

Do you want to be able to truly love yourself?

Then learn to pursue the one who is love Himself.

Recognising the Gold that we carry as individuals is where we must start. Unless we attribute the same value to ourselves as God does … unless we learn how to be less critical of ourselves and more loving … until we become less frustrated with ourselves and more patient … we will never be able to go out and do the same for others.

The answers to the questions we have about our validity and worth in life will never be answered by accolades or possessions, only by the words of Jesus Christ Himself.

So, what is He saying?

Post it notes!

As a teenager, I remember my dad coming home from work one day armed with his latest idea to help motivate my brother and I to *actually do* the things we were asked to do, *when we were asked to do them*. This was not something we were very good at!

I imagine he must have been on some kind of time management training course. He arrived home the proud owner of a huge pad of sticky Post-it notes. Every individual little square had the words "DO IT NOW" plastered across it.

In the weeks that followed, every time Dad or Mum asked us to do something, like unpacking the dishwasher, and we would respond with our customary, "Yeah, in a minute!" Dad would pull out his pad of Post-It notes. Attaching one to the front of the dishwasher as visible confirmation of his words, he would declare,

"No, do it now!"

In no time those Post-it notes were literally everywhere: in the kitchen, our bedrooms, even in the downstairs loo! It became more than a little irritating, especially given my naturally surly teenage disposition. Over time, however, the notes began to take effect. Eventually, when asked to do something, we would find ourselves saying,

"Yeah, in a … [sigh] … OK, I'll do it now!!!"

Although at the time I really didn't appreciate the approach, in retrospect I'm very grateful to my dad for his passionate use of Post-it notes! It was a model lesson in renewing the mind.

The constant visual reminder to "Do it now", along with his persuasive verbal reinforcement, changed my ingrained "do it later" mind set to a "do it now" one.

This may all sound a bit trivial, but actually this discipline helped to form a new foundation in my life. Today, those three words still echo in my head whenever a household chore confronts me. I'm sure my dad thought it was simply a creative way of galvanising my brother and I into action, but actually he was changing the way I thought.

The process of being transformed by the truth of God's Word is very similar. Paul writes in Romans 12:2 about being *transformed by the renewing of your mind.* The more we are exposed to the words that God says about us, the more they will change us from the inside out.

Scripture is very clear when it comes to describing how our Father in heaven sees us (at the end of this chapter there is a list of some of these amazing statements). When we begin to understand just how precious we are in God's eyes, and the more we come into agreement with what He says about us, allowing it to take root in our hearts, the more fruit it will bear.

God's opinion of you is the only one that truly matters. Your identity is not rooted in what you have or haven't done, but solely in the truth of who He says you are. We need to listen to His voice above all others.

Over the years I have taken to sticking pieces of paper all over my house with such "truth statements" written on them. They are simple declarations of what my Heavenly Father says about me. I stick them on my hall mirror, kitchen cabinets, or on doors – anywhere I will walk past them and notice. They are visual reminders of the words God is speaking to me about who I am in His eyes. Often, I will speak the words out loud, agreeing with what the Father is saying.

The power of agreement

I am a strong believer in the creative power of the spoken word. We know that at the inception of creation, God spoke.

> *Then God **said**, "Let there be light" and there was light.* (Genesis 1:3)

God **spoke**... and substance was created.

As God's children, made in His image, we carry the same creative power inside us. We carry the Spirit of the Creator Himself. Therefore, when we speak, things are brought into being.

Let's be sensible for a minute. This doesn't mean we can just think of anything we want and magically speak it into being. That would be ridiculous!

When my son was about 8 years old, he heard me give a talk on the creative power of the spoken word. He thought this was fantastic and the next night, as he was getting ready for bed, I found him standing in the middle of his bedroom speaking into being a new PlayStation for himself! I had to gently explain that it doesn't work quite like that.

As an aside, at one point he thought the Holy Spirit was like "the force" (he was a huge Star Wars fan) and he stood beside me one Sunday morning as I was leading the church meeting, with his hand outstretched, trying to use the force on the congregation. He was deeply disappointed when he found he couldn't lift them all up in the air and make them fly backwards. Got to love him for trying though!

No, we can't just "create" whatever we want. We can, however, come into agreement with what God is saying and doing in Heaven, align ourselves with it, and begin to speak it out. When we do, something is created; something powerful begins to happen.

> *You will also decree a thing and it will be established for you.* (Job 22:28 NASB)

So much negativity is at large in the world that we need to become militant with the truth. We need to be intentional in declaring it, over and over. We are not victims of our past. We are not bound by the things others have spoken over us. We are not ruled by the lies the enemy has whispered into the deep places of our hearts.

The truth is, we are overcomers. We have been bought with a price. Freedom, joy, peace and love are all available to us, at all times. They are found only in Jesus and we are established in them through Him alone. All we need to do is to break agreement with the whispering lies of the enemy and instead, intentionally come into agreement with Him who is truth. To agree with His word, speak it out, then live it out.

Maybe it's time to go out and buy yourself a pack of Post-it notes?

Get to work and begin to mine for the Gold that your Creator has put inside you. If you don't know where to begin, here are a few helpful scriptures to get you started.

I am chosen by Him. (1 Thessalonians 1:14)
I am greatly loved. (1 John 3:3)
I am His child, I am a joint heir with Jesus. (Romans 8:17)

I am redeemed and forgiven. (Colossians 1:14)

I am not condemned, I have been set free. (Romans 8:1-2)

I am more than a conqueror through Christ who loves me. (Romans 8:37)

I do not have a spirit of fear, but of love, power and a sound mind. (2 Timothy 1:7)

I have the mind of Christ. (1 Corinthians 2:16)

He has given me peace. (John 14:27)

He gives me joy. (Romans 15:13)

I can boldly approach His throne, with great confidence. (Hebrews 4:16)

I have direct access to God Himself. (Ephesians 2:18)

He has anointed me. (2 Corinthians 1:21)

I have been chosen to bear much fruit. (John 15:16)

Until we begin to accept, understand and recognise the Gold we carry as individuals, giving it the value it deserves, we will be hindered from doing the same for others.

Learn to mine for Gold in your own life first. Then you will be free to mine for it in the lives of your friends, family, community, nation and beyond.

4. The Small and Insignificant

"The truth is, it doesn't matter how small or insignificant you think you are … it's not about you … it's about Him, who He is, and what He can do through you."

There is a story in the Gospel of John that over the years has become a favourite of mine. I've lost count of the times that Jesus has brought me back to it in one way or another. I'm not sure if this is because I'm very slow on the uptake and He is trying to teach me something I'm still not getting – or whether it's simply because this story expresses so well how I feel on a regular basis.

Between you and me I'm hoping it's the latter!

> *When Jesus looked up and saw a great crowd coming toward him, he said to Philip, "Where shall we buy bread for these people to eat?" He asked this only to test him, for he already had in mind what he was going to do.*
>
> *Philip answered him, "It would take more than half a year's wages to buy enough bread for each one to have a bite!"*

Another of his disciples, Andrew, Simon Peter's brother, spoke up, "Here is a boy with five small barley loaves and two small fish, but how far will they go among so many?"

Jesus said, "Have the people sit down." There was plenty of grass in that place, and they sat down (about five thousand men were there). Jesus then took the loaves, gave thanks, and distributed to those who were seated as much as they wanted. He did the same with the fish.

When they had all had enough to eat, he said to his disciples, "Gather the pieces that are left over. Let nothing be wasted." So they gathered them and filled twelve baskets with the pieces of the five barley loaves left over by those who had eaten. (John 6:5 NIV)

It was a seemingly impossible situation that Jesus and the disciples found themselves in that day. More than five thousand hungry people, not including women and children, needed feeding and all that was available was a tiny amount of food.

There were no supermarkets nearby, no fancy coffee shops or catering companies in the local vicinity. There was no local artisan baker near the mountainside who could help out and provide what they needed. They were in the middle of nowhere with practically nothing in their hands.

As Jesus sees the hungry masses in front of Him, He turns to His friend Philip and asks him a question:

"Where shall we buy bread for these people to eat?"

In other words,

"How are we going to solve this problem, Philip? How will we feed these people?"

Philip was an amazing disciple. Known as "the evangelist" he was a man of great faith. By this time he had spent a lot of time with Jesus and had seen Him do many mind-blowing things: healings, miracles and more besides. Knowing this, his response to Jesus both fascinates and surprises me. He simply says,

"Six months' wages won't buy enough bread for everyone to eat and have a bite!"

Looked at from one perspective he was quite right. His assessment of the situation was factually accurate and correct. But then another answer came along.

Here is a boy, holding in his hands five small barley loaves and two small fish. Both Jesus and His disciples see the boy, but how they respond to him is completely different.

The disciples see the loaves and fish and say,

"How far will that go among so many?"

Jesus sees the loaves and fish and says,

"Perfect! Have the people sit down, ready to eat!"

Jesus rejects the natural wisdom of the situation. In fact, He rejects the obvious "facts" regarding what can be done with such a small amount of food, compared to such a large number of people. Ignoring these barriers, He goes to the boy and receives his tiny lunch offering. He takes hold of it and says,

"This is exactly what I am going to use!"

He takes the small offering that appears so insignificant, the tiny amount of food that is clearly not enough, and He creates something miraculous, beautiful and abundant from it.

AMAZING!

Chickens, chickens, chickens

I remember the first time our ministry ever saw the multiplication of food. It was Christmastime. We had decided to throw a huge banquet feast for everyone who lived in a particular slum community we'd been working in.

We hardly had any money, but were determined to make it as lavish as possible. We invited everyone who lived in the community to come along and set up camp outside the local "church hall", which was actually a makeshift building constructed from iron sheets.

One of the team came up with the idea of giving the gift of a chicken to each of the slum families who came along, so they could enjoy a chicken feast on Christmas Day. Meat was a very rare luxury for most of our families and chicken was considered to be the most luxurious meat of all! I thought it sounded like a great idea and promptly asked a member of my team to order 200 chickens, to be delivered on the day of the event.

I don't know what happened to my brain the day I ordered the chickens, but something clearly misfired. I didn't think about the fact that our families had no access to electricity, let alone refrigerators in their homes (they live in mud huts for goodness sake!). They would have no way of storing a dead bird and ensuring it stayed fresh until the big day. None of this registered in my mind as I ordered those 200 chickens … until afterwards!

Fortunately, one of our staff members instinctively understood the dilemma and had placed the order for me. Imagine my surprise then, when subsequently a van arrived with 200 *live* chickens, all squawking and flapping in the back!

The mamas and children found the hour and a half it took for my husband, my team and I to hand over these live, biting, noisy gifts one by one, extremely entertaining!

Prior to this gift-giving ceremony we provided the villagers with a meal. Despite our limited budget we wanted to provide the nicest meal possible, so with the help of some wonderful ladies from the community, we prepared a meal consisting of matoke (green bananas), beef, beans and rice.

Everything was carefully planned and we knew that as long as we were sensible with the portion sizes, we had just about enough to feed the number of people we had invited. The problem was, word got around very quickly that free food was being handed out in the local church hall. Within an hour of the festivities beginning we had way more "attendees" than we'd been expecting!

I instructed my team to begin to serve the food up and to be "moderate" with what they put on each plate. My understanding of "moderate" turned out to be quite different from that of my Ugandan staff members! It wasn't long before I saw mamas and children sitting down to feast on plates of food that looked like mini-mountains!

After we had served everyone, I went to check how much food was left, expecting to find little if any leftovers. To my amazement, there was almost as much as when we'd begun. This being the case, we invited anyone who was still hungry to come up for seconds. The whole place came back for more and so we served everyone again.

Even after this second round of serving, still a huge amount of food remained! We asked if anyone wanted thirds, but this time there were no takers, so we picked up our enormous saucepans and walked around the neighbouring village, giving out food to anyone who wanted it.

People came to us with all sorts of containers, from buckets to jerry cans. Those who didn't have containers simply brought plastic bags. We kept pouring the food in until eventually the people stopped coming and our team were exhausted.

Only then did the food promptly run out.

Astonishing!

This has been our testimony for the last 10 years. Time and again we have seen Jesus come and take the little we had to give Him – our insignificant "fives loaves and two fish" – and He has filled it with Himself, so that something beautiful and transformational begins to take place.

Mighty warrior

Judges chapter 6 recounts the story of Gideon. We meet him as he is hiding out in a wine press. Gideon is not your Hollywood hero type. Far from it. He's the polar opposite: scared, jumpy and hiding from his enemies who are encamped all around him. He is hoping he won't be discovered, fearing for his life.

Wine presses were generally dug deep into the ground. If you climbed inside a wine press you would be out of sight of everyone. No one, including your enemies, would know you were there. Frightened Gideon is doing his best to keep out of danger, minding his own business, quietly threshing some wheat for his family, when the Angel of the Lord appears to him and says,

"The Lord is with you, mighty warrior."

In my mind's eye I imagine this as a great announcement: a trumpet sounds and there is a blinding white light. None of this is written in the story, but it feels as though a statement of such enormity warrants it!

What do you think Gideon thinks at this moment?

"Mighty Warrior? What me?"

I wonder if he looked around the room, expecting to see someone else the angel was addressing? Confirming that he was, in fact, alone, and the angel was speaking to him, he responded by saying (as the NIV translation puts it),

"Pardon me, my Lord?"

We might say,

"Excuse me? Are you kidding? I think you've got the wrong person. Who is it you're looking for?"

Ignoring his confusion, the angel speaks again and tells Gideon he is being sent out on a heavenly assignment. God is going to use *him* to bring deliverance to a whole nation.

Thinking the angel must be confused, Gideon responds the same way – *Pardon me?* – and then proceeds to list all the reasons why this cannot possibly be true.

He says things like, "My clan is the weakest and I am the least of all the people in my family." In other words,

"YOU'VE GOT THE WRONG PERSON!"

Have you ever felt like you are the "wrong person" in a challenging situation?

I know I have. I often have days when I feel too small and too insignificant. I feel as though I am not gifted enough, clever enough or brave enough to do what I believe God is telling me to do.

What I love about Gideon's story is that the Lord sees past all that Gideon says about himself. God ignores his fear, doubt and insecurity. Instead, He simply calls Gideon by his true identity.

Gideon says, "I am weak."

The Lord says, "I call you mighty."

God goes one step further. He tells Gideon to go and bring deliverance to a whole nation, with the beautiful promise in verse 16 that,

"I will be with you."

Gideon says, "I can't."

The Lord replies, "You can, because I can, and I will be with you."

Now jump forward in the story to verse 34 – my favourite verse of the whole passage. Gideon's enemies begin to join forces and are closing in on him. An enormous army prepares to march against Gideon and his men. As Gideon gets ready to face the biggest battle of his life, verse 34 simply says,

"Then the Spirit of the Lord came on Gideon." (NIV)

Or as the NLT version puts it,

"Then the Spirit of the Lord *took possession* of Gideon."

The original Hebrew words translated into English for us, literally mean "The Spirit of the Lord *clothed himself with Gideon*" or "The Spirit of the Lord *put Gideon on like a glove*."

Isn't that stunning?

The Lord takes Gideon and "puts him on", filling him completely. As a result, suddenly everything changes.

Take possession

A few years back I was worshipping in my bedroom, enjoying spending time with Jesus. My family were all out for the day, I had a rare few hours to myself, and I was making the most of it.

Despite the fact that I am most definitely not the world's best singer, I love to worship and I love to worship loudly! So there

I was, lying on my bed, singing at the top of my voice, when suddenly I had a vision.

I had been reading the story of Gideon earlier that week and I was inspired. I wanted to have the same experience as he did – I wanted the Holy Spirit to come and wear me like a glove. I began to shout at the top of my voice, "Come and possess me Jesus … come and take every part of me."

I was so desperate for more of Him.

It was then that the vision began to unfold.

I saw Jesus walk into my bedroom and stand at the foot of my bed. I was overwhelmed at His nearness and noticed straight away that He had in His hand what looked like a dagger.

I assumed that the weapon was symbolic – that it meant He wanted to go to battle over something. I decided it must mean He was calling me to go to war in prayer over something. I asked Him,

"What is it you want me to do? What is it you want me to pray?"

As soon as I finished speaking, He walked round to the side of my bed and raised His hand, holding the dagger high in the air.

What happened next shocked me to my core.

As I lay there on the bed, my arms stretched out, Jesus took that dagger and plunged it deep into my chest.

I was stunned!

He then proceeded to slice open my stomach from top to bottom. After that He did the same with each arm and each leg, slicing my skin open.

Then, slowly, He began to peel back my skin, until my whole body was laid open and you could see my flesh and blood and bones. It was shocking. So unexpected and disturbing. Then He climbed onto the bed and lay down on top me. Immediately, my skin began to seal over the top of Him until He was encased inside me.

Finally, I got it. It was a visual demonstration of the truth of Galatians 2:20.

My old self has been crucified with Christ. It is no longer I who live, but Christ who lives in me.

Am I saying that I am Jesus?

Absolutely not! That would be ridiculous.

What I am saying is that I am carrier of Him. I carry His life, His love, His peace, His presence, everywhere I go.

This is the truth: it doesn't matter how small or insignificant you think you are, because it's not about you, it's all about Him. The point of the Gospel is that it's all about who He is and what He can do for you.

It doesn't matter how ill-equipped you think you are or how insignificant you feel. Living out the abundant life to which God has called you does not depend on what you can or can't do. It only matters who He is and what He can do through you.

When we live our lives fully yielded to Him, in total abandon and surrender, He comes and inhabits the small offering of ourselves, then something beautiful and powerful begins to happen.

When we understand what it is that we carry, the treasure, the Gold within, suddenly everything changes.

You see, it means that when I reach out my hand and lay it on someone who is sick, His hand reaches out too.

When I walk into a room, He walks in there with me.

When I speak, His voice can be heard.

Just think about that for a moment. You have a treasure in your jar of clay.

You are packed full of Gold.

Do you realise the potential you carry to change your world?

But we have this treasure in jars of clay to show that this all-surpassing power is from God and not from us. We are hard pressed on every side, but not crushed; perplexed, but not in despair; persecuted, but not abandoned; struck down, but not destroyed. We always carry around in our body the death of Jesus, so that the life of Jesus may also be revealed in our body. For we who are alive are always being given over to death for Jesus' sake, so that his life may also be revealed in our mortal body.

(2 Corinthians 4:7)

5. Out of the Ashes

"You have a choice to make. You can be ruled by your circumstances and what the world says about them, or you can live in alignment with Jesus and what He says about them."

Perspectives

In the previous chapters I have spoken about the difference between how we see and speak about ourselves, and how God sees and speaks about us. More often than not, our opinions are completely contrary to His. The same applies to the situations we encounter in life; the circumstances we find ourselves in. Often, we have one view, but God sees things completely differently.

Over the years, living in Africa, we have experienced many of the same atrocities other parts of the world have suffered: terrorist attacks, suicide bombs detonated in shopping malls, the constant threat of random violence. After a while it became commonplace for us to receive alerts from the British High Commission, urging us to be extra vigilant due to the high level of risk.

It's easy to become a little immune to such warnings after a while, but one Wednesday the reality hit home. My young daughter arrived home from school, dropped her bag by the kitchen door as usual, and made her way straight for the snack cupboard.

We did our usual thing. I asked her, "How was your day?" and she replied with the standard, "Fine." Then, as she turned to head to her bedroom, she paused and added,

"Oh, we did do this new thing called *terrorism drill* this afternoon."

"Terrorism drill?"

I hardly knew how to respond to this as my thoughts ran in every direction. I was relieved when she just continued chatting and explained what had happened.

She described, in great detail, a scenario they had played out and "practiced" for at school. They were told to imagine that armed men had broken into the compound and begun a shooting spree. The children had then practiced keeping low on the floor, staying away from windows, padlocking themselves into cupboards, and tried to breathe without making a sound, so that no one would know they were there.

I absorbed all this information. This wasn't something I had ever considered one of my children would talk about, let alone experience. I thought back to my own schooldays in a quiet little English school, where the most exciting event we experienced was the annual fire drill. We would all stand on the playing field, laughing and joking while the teacher took the register.

Now, the things that made up our daily African life were Ebola outbreaks, AIDS infection, political riots and terrorism threats. Distant, far-removed things I'd previously only heard about on the BBC World News were now a day-to-day reality.

As I stood there listening to my daughter talk about her day, I asked myself several questions:

What should be my response to these events?

Should I stop my daughter from attending the school she loves, simply out of fear of something that might happen? It was very tempting.

What were we doing here? What on earth was I thinking, raising my children in such a place?

There were definitely times when I wondered if we had lost the plot. Why wake up each morning to start yet another day in a country full of uncertainty and threat?

This was certainly one of those days.

Later that evening, after the children were in bed, I took some time to talk with the Lord about all that had happened and He began to challenge me. In answer to my many questions, the Lord responded with some of His own and challenged me to think...

When I am surrounded by difficult circumstances, by trials and challenges, what is it that I focus on?

What or who is it that I put my trust in?

What is my anchor?

Do I accept what appears to be the "truth" of my situation – that which I see with my natural eyes?

Or is there something else – *someone else* – I can trust in? An even greater truth. The truth of who God is and what He is saying and doing.

Death to life

Later that evening, the Lord led me to the familiar passage of Scripture in Mark 15.

> *At noon, darkness fell across the whole land until three o'clock. Then at three o'clock Jesus called out with a loud voice, "My God, my God, why have you abandoned me?"*
>
> *Some of the bystanders misunderstood and thought he was calling for the prophet Elijah. One of them ran and filled a sponge with sour wine, holding it up to him on a reed stick so he could drink.*
>
> *"Wait!" he said. "Let's see whether Elijah comes to take him down!"*
>
> *Then Jesus uttered another loud cry and breathed his last. And the curtain in the sanctuary of the Temple was torn in two, from top to bottom.*
>
> *When the Roman officer who stood facing him saw how he had died, he exclaimed, "This man truly was the Son of God!"*

As I read these words again, I took time to imagine myself into the scene. I wanted to be *in the story*. I pictured myself as one of Jesus' disciples and saw myself there, standing amidst the crowd that had gathered. I imagined looking at the cross, looking around at the hillside, the faces of the crowd, the soldiers positioned around…

What were the people saying to one another? What were they whispering?

I imagined the looks on the face of my friends as we stood, together, watching our friend and Lord die.

And then … hearing Jesus let out a loud cry and die. What would I have felt during that moment?

The disciples couldn't see into the future. They had no idea Jesus was going to be resurrected in a few days; that they would get to speak to Him again. Presently they were witnessing the death of the one person they had put all their hope in. Jesus was the one they had trusted more than anyone; the one they had given up everything to follow. They loved Him, the supposed Messiah, who was now hanging there, dead!

They were confused, frightened, devastated. They were broken-hearted, hopeless and abandoned. So, what now…?

I understood what Father God was saying to me. The things we see happening around us, or to us in life is not the full picture or the end of the story. God understands the bigger picture, the grand narrative of our lives, according to His plans and purposes. What looks like an end is often a beginning … if only we would trust.

What we understand of our circumstances is rarely the whole truth of the situation.

What appeared to the disciples as death and failure was the exact opposite. It was life and hope being released to all generations.

Understanding this in a fresh light led me to ask myself some more questions:

What reality was I living out of?
What truth was I aligning myself with?
And where did I put my trust?

Crisis

In April of 2012 my husband, Simon, was taken ill very suddenly. Although I knew he was unwell at the time, I had no clue as to the severity of his condition.

We took him to our local medical centre, where he was looked after for a few days. They did the best they could to get him well, but to cut a long story short it wasn't working. Quite suddenly, one morning, we realized that Simon was critically ill and needed immediate surgery.

There was no hospital in Uganda with the necessary skills to carry out the level of surgery Simon required, so with only hours' notice, we were put in an ambulance and rushed to the airport, where an air ambulance was waiting to fly us to a hospital in Nairobi, Kenya. As soon as we arrived in Nairobi, the plan was to take Simon straight into theatre.

That journey was one of the most surreal experiences of my life and certainly one I hoped I'd never have to repeat. The air ambulance was well-equipped and even had a full-sized hospital bed for Simon to lie down on. As soon as we boarded the medics began to work on him, doing all they could to keep him alive and get him to Nairobi.

I sat on a small seat next to his bed and looked on helplessly. At one point I felt so overwhelmed by the situation that I had to look away, pressing my face to one of the small windows, trying to compose myself and hold it all together. I didn't know what to do. As I stared out of the window, I could see lions below, wandering the African plains, while my husband was lying next to me fighting for his life.

Is this really happening now? I thought.

Eventually we arrived in Nairobi and Simon was rushed straight into theatre. I was left standing outside with my anxieties and no idea what would happen next.

I will never forget the kindness of the nursing staff there. They cared for Simon so well. The surgery was a success and he appeared to make a steady recovery. After nearly two weeks of rest, our medical insurance company flew us back to the UK to reunite us with our children, who had already travelled back with their grandparents.

Over the following days and weeks of Simon's recovery, we were asked countless times,

"Is that it, then?"

In other words, "Are you done with Africa?" though no one ever said those exact words. People wondered if the scare with Simon had pushed us over the edge, convincing us to move back to the West and … what? "Safety"? "Normality"?

Every time we were asked that question, our answer was the same. Were we done?

"Of course not!"

It was far too late for that. Jesus had taken our hearts captive for the nation of Uganda. We couldn't un-see what we had seen. We couldn't close our eyes and pretend the poverty, suffering and injustice we'd witnessed in Africa didn't exist – because it did! We could not, therefore, ignore it. We couldn't pretend it had all gone away and close our hearts and minds to it.

That wasn't an option. The thought never even crossed our minds. Yes, we had days in Africa where everything felt just too difficult, too costly, and we longed for the familiar comforts of our old life in England. Yes, we had days where we wondered if we had the strength and courage to carry on. When you hold a tiny child in your arms and have to watch them die of a disease that is totally curable in the West, it hurts; it costs; it breaks your heart and it can be overwhelming.

But walk away? No, we couldn't do that.

Africa had become our home. The people living in the slums had become our family. We were desperate to get back to them.

But more than all of that, the Lord Himself had made it very clear to us that our time in Africa was not over. We *needed* to return.

The next few months were taken up with the slow process of recovery – for Simon, physically, and for all us mentally, following the trauma of his illness. After three months we received the "all clear" from the doctors and flew home to Uganda.

Here we go again

A couple of months later I was sat in my garden. It is one of my favourite places in the world to be. I love to sit there at the end of a busy day in the slum. With a cup of tea in my hand, watching the clouds roll by and enjoying the heat of the African sun on my face, the noise of Kampala buzzes all around me.

On this day I was sat in my favourite corner of the garden, under a shady palm tree, having just returned from talking with a local witchdoctor about who Jesus is, when my son came running out of the house. He had found his dad unconscious on the bathroom floor.

I ran into the house and sure enough, Simon was out cold. It didn't take long for him to come around, but when he did, he was in considerable pain. Minutes later we found ourselves back in our car, rushing him across Kampala to the doctors.

To our shock we soon discovered that he needed another major surgery to save his life. This time, however, there wasn't enough time to fly us to the hospital in Nairobi. He would have to have surgery at a local clinic in Kampala.

The facilities were crude and basic, but the staff did the best they could with what they had. Once again, I was so thankful for their skill, love and care as they performed the surgery successfully and Simon's life was saved, again.

This time Simon didn't seem to recover fully from the trauma of the surgery and remained seriously ill and in an enormous amount of pain for the next six weeks. His body was fighting an infection that would just not go away. Eventually the decision was made to fly him back to the UK for further investigation. Back in England, he spent the next four months in and out hospital and underwent three more surgical procedures, all of which were unsuccessful.

Throughout this season I spent a lot of time flying back and forth between the UK and Uganda. It was an incredibly challenging time for our family. At times it was very scary and constantly exhausting.

In the November of that year, a surgeon took me to one side to explain the situation to me: Simon needed yet more surgery and he needed it soon. Without it, he assured me, he would most likely die. An added complication, however, was that his level of infection and weakened state gave the staff concerns that he wouldn't be able to survive the surgery.

We were left with an impossible decision to make. The medical experts suggested that they try to get Simon as physically strong as possible, then they would operate. There really was no other option.

We knew that the surgery would mean another long period of recovery, so my son and I made a quick trip back to Uganda to set things in place, ready for us to be away from our missions base for an extended period.

A couple of days after we arrived in Africa, however, I received a phone call. Simon's health had begun to go rapidly downhill. The surgeons couldn't wait any longer. They wanted to operate immediately.

I spoke to one of the nurses who had been caring for Simon so lovingly and asked her to tell me the reality of the situation. No diplomacy – just give me the truth. She replied honestly suggesting I prepare myself for the worst, saying I should take some time to speak to Simon on the phone and say anything I wanted to say. In other words … goodbye.

My mum went to Simon's bedside and held her mobile next to his head. He was unable to speak, so I told him simply that I loved him, that I was on my way, and that he did NOT have permission to die on me that day! My son and I then raced to the airport and caught the first flight back to London.

As I sat on the plane a few hours later, unsure whether my husband would be dead or alive by the time I arrived, a thousand scenarios flooded my mind and I thought I was going to be sick, faint, or both.

I looked at my teenage son and wondered how I would raise him without his dad. How would our lives work without Simon? What impact would it have on both my children? Our family unit? Our ministry?

The longer I allowed the thoughts to swirl, the more I was drowning in fear. I gripped the arms of my seat and concentrated on breathing slowly and not freaking out. I knew I had a decision to make right there and then…

Was I going to allow myself to be consumed by the painful circumstances I found myself in, or choose to shift my focus? Would I keep my eyes on the difficult situation, or shift my gaze onto Jesus and the reality of who He is and what He was speaking about this situation?

With all my strength I chose to do the second.

Sitting in that crowded plane I began to worship. I sang every song I could think of that would be a declaration of God's love, goodness and faithfulness.

Here is the truth: regardless of what is happening in our life, God does not change. His character remains constant. He is present with us in every moment that life throws our way. His love, faithfulness, kindness, grace and compassion never fails or falters.

Our circumstances do not get to define who He is. Instead, *who He is* defines our circumstances!

Please hear me on this: I am not suggesting we should naïvely pretend our challenges in life aren't real, bury our heads in the sand, and hope they magically go away. Quite the opposite! We must learn how to look our challenges in the face, acknowledge they are real, and then look up. We must lift our heads, fix our gaze on Jesus, and listen to what He is saying in that moment. Jesus must be our anchor. He is the reality that is *above* every situation and circumstance.

Looking back, I am so thankful for the lessons the Lord taught me through this season of life. Given the choice, would

I choose to live it again? Absolutely NOT! But I am grateful for all the things God taught our family and the kindness He showed us as we walked through it all.

Simon survived his surgery. His life really is a miracle and not a day goes by when he isn't aware of what a gift it is to wake up each morning and to simply breathe.

That season changed a lot of things for us. We learnt so much about ourselves, about grace, about the kindness of the Lord in the deep messiness of life and about His uncompromising faithfulness to us, even in the face of our own doubts, failures and inconsistencies.

Beauty out of ashes

Sometimes in life our problems can seem huge, the things that surround us so big, and their reality so convincing.

For Jesus' disciples, that day at the cross was a trial of their faith. The truth of their circumstances looked bleak. Everything was dark, confusing and scary.

But there was a greater reality at work; a greater truth unfolding.

The disciples saw one reality … death. The greater reality was that the power of death was being broken forever. Life, freedom, healing and hope were being released to all future generations.

When you are in the midst of turmoil it is difficult to see the bigger plan of God. It's hard to understand that He is right there with you.

During our tough season, I clearly remember one evening, after a particularly hard day, where I was just exhausted. I felt overwhelmed and defeated, unsure how I could keep going. Amidst tears, I whispered to the Lord,

"Everywhere I look, all I can see are the ashes of our lives."

Immediately the words left my lips, the Lord replied:

"Nicola, when you look at something and all you see are ashes, I look at it and see something different. I see potential – the potential to form something beautiful! Because that's what I do: I make beauty out of ashes."

I wept as, once again, I realized that my perspective and Jesus' perspective are so very different. I needed to realign my vision with His.

In His faithfulness, Jesus took all our brokenness, pain and confusion and did just that – formed something beautiful out of it – and He will do the same for you.

It's what He does and who He is. He can't help Himself! He is a redeemer and is constantly working out His stunningly redemptive plan for our lives, forming beauty from our ashes. In other words, creating Gold.

Does the "beauty" He promises always look like we think it should? No.

Does the process of beautification always happen how we think it should? No.

Does transformation and redemption always happen according to our timing? No.

For the disciples that day at the cross, did the Messiah look like they expected Him to? No.

Did the events of that day make sense to them in that moment? No.

Did they understand what was happening? No.

Could Jesus have healed my husband in an instant? Yes, of course He could. Did He? No, He didn't. Do I understand why? If I am honest, no, not really!

We cannot guess at the reasons why God doesn't do what we expect. But what I can tell you for sure is this:

Whatever is going on in your life, whatever is happening to you or around you…

He is always trustworthy.

He is always faithful.

He is always good.

He is always love.

You have a choice to make. You can be ruled by your circumstances and what the world says about them, or you can live in alignment with Jesus and what He says about them.

You need to decide to live from a different place, with a different perspective – the perspective of the unchanging character of the God who loves you and paid the ultimate price to save you.

Lay down your human understanding of your challenging circumstances and root yourself in Him. Listen to His voice and His truth.

To see your life from God's perspective is to see *potential*, to see *beauty*, to see *Gold*.

> *Trust in the Lord with all your heart and lean not on your own understanding; in all your ways submit to him and he will make your paths straight.* (Proverbs 3:5-6 NIV)

6. To the Ends of the Earth

"If you choose to look a little further … beyond the seen into the unseen, you will find a depth of beauty there so raw, so resilient and real, that it will take your breath away … poverty wears many different faces and carries many different disguises."

The communities where we love and serve around the world are often messy, broken places. Recently I was on a video call with the Director of our newly emerging missions base in Rwanda and she was filling me in on all that she had been doing.

The week prior to our call had been Genocide Memorial Week and she had received the great honour of being invited to join in with the memorial activities in a local community.

She began to explain to me how she had sat with many families and heard their stories of how the genocide had affected them. They were stories of great suffering and brutal violence. As their harrowing tales began to draw to a close, they asked if she would like to then join them in visiting the church where the massacre in that area had taken place.

Of course, she said yes.

As she entered the church building, she realised immediately that the room had not been touched since the day the attack had taken place. Scattered across the floor were the skeletons, clothes and shoes of the men, women and children whose lives had been taken so violently. The walls and ceiling were stained with their spilt blood.

As I listened to her recount all that she had seen and heard that day, I found it hard to take it all in. This was the story of one small village, but it represented the horrors experienced by a whole nation. Horrors that you and I can barely imagine.

It would be easy to look at communities like these with our natural eyes, listen to their stories, and feel completely overwhelmed by the pain and suffering of these people. We might wonder, *is there really any hope for them?* We could question whether there is really any love strong enough to heal the pain of their past; a redemption powerful enough to bring the reconciliation and restoration that is needed. We might just write them off as too damaged and broken.

Here in the UK we are facing our own challenges right now. Not genocide or ethnic cleansing, but families who are hard pressed to navigate life on a daily basis. Parents who are wondering where the money for their family's next meal is coming from, dependent on the kindness and provision of local food banks. We have a health system that is stretched to breaking point, with constantly limited resources, struggling to provide the right care for those who need it. Then there are the issues of drug and alcohol abuse, gang-related gun and knife crime, thousands struggling with their mental health, self-harm and suicide, and more.

The news networks bring us stories of terrorist attacks in major cities like London and Manchester, or in nearby countries like France, Belgium and Germany. Further afield there are situations that seem out of control in countries like Syria; humanitarian crises on a massive scale in places like Yemen and South Sudan; a global refugee crisis on an enormous scale, such that the world is struggling to know how to respond.

These are just some of the headlines.

Banda

I remember the first time I walked into Banda Slum. We had driven past this community many times, as it was on the main road into the city centre. Each time we drove by, it felt like there was some kind of magnetic pull on my heart; as if it was drawing me to itself. I felt completely captured by a community I had never even met.

We decided that we needed to talk to the local leaders there and ask for permission to go in. Each slum community has its own elected "council" which is responsible for the area, and culture dictates that before a ministry like ours begins to serve there, it is necessary to meet with the leaders and ask their permission. I spoke to a contact of mine and he said he would set up a meeting.

At this time, we were still a very small team and were only working in two small communities in Uganda. We had few resources and little money in our bank account.

Viewed from the road, however, the Banda community appeared fairly small, so I didn't think it was unrealistic for us to serve there too.

I was wrong about that!

The day came for us to meet the local leaders. I remember climbing into our little 4x4 with such excitement and expectation. I had been dreaming of this day for over a year and I couldn't wait to get started.

The drive from our home took less than fifteen minutes and immediately upon arriving at the agreed meeting place, just outside the community itself, we were warmly welcomed. Someone fetched a small wooden bench for us to sit on and a cup of chai was placed in each of our hands before we were introduced to everyone.

I always love meeting new people and this day was no exception. Long introductions took place as we learnt all about the men and women who were overseeing the slum. Then my team and I briefly introduced ourselves and explained our hearts to serve them and their slum dwellers.

Our enthusiasm was returned in kind and we were asked if we'd like to go in and walk around the area. We said yes, and off we went.

As we walked along the dirt road, making our way in, I turned to the main leader and asked,

"So roughly how many people live in this community?"

I was expecting him to reply with a number in the low thousands. I was shocked when he replied,

"Oh, about 1 million."

I nearly passed out! My mouth went dry and my heart began to pound. What had I done? How on earth had I not realised how huge this place actually was? And what on earth had I got us into?

He went on to explain how the community was broken down into individual zones for the sake of easier management. He then asked me which zone I wanted to go to.

"Take me to the poorest zone of all," I replied.

He looked slightly confused and double checked, then triple checked, that I really did want to go there. I assured him that I did, at which he sighed and said,

"OK, follow me."

The rest of that afternoon was overwhelming to say the least. We walked around meeting the people who lived there, greeting families, visiting bars and brothels, being introduced to the resident witchdoctors, and heard story after story of violence, poverty and pain. My heart was undone.

It doesn't take long to realise how desperate life in the slums is. The moment you step in you experience sensory overload. There is death, disease, poverty and malnutrition everywhere you look. There is simply no escape from it. Not only are the people living in desperate circumstances, but there is no getting away – they are trapped there. All of the slum families we know live hand to mouth, each day hoping they will earn enough money to feed their family that evening. Some days they are successful and some days they are not.

We were used to working in such places, we had been doing it for years, but to be honest we had never seen anything on this scale. The magnitude of it literally took my breath away.

Whether there was actually a million people living there, it was impossible to tell, but it was by far the biggest community we had seen, and we'd only visited one small part of it.

We finished our walk up by an old railway line. From that vantage point you could see the whole of the zone stretched out across reclaimed swamp land. I will never forget standing there that afternoon, looking down at the enormity of what was before me. A vast number of people trapped in a lifestyle of poverty and all that comes with it. I asked myself the inevitable questions:

What on earth could our small team do with the scant resources we had?
Would we make any difference to these people's lives?
Was it possible?
Should we even try?

It would have been very easy to look at the size of the problem that lay in front of us and decide it was just too big. Who were we to think we could make a difference? Maybe it was better for everyone for us to simply walk away?

To be honest it was incredibly tempting. This was a very violent community. It had a deeply embedded history of witchcraft and drug abuse. It was a very intimidating place to be.

But, it was too late for that. We had seen it. Now we had a responsibility to respond.

Hidden beauty

What struck me most the first time I walked through a slum was the lack of colour and vibrancy that is seen in so many other parts of Africa. There were mud huts, mud walls, mud floors and mud rivers. Mud, as far as the eye could see.

There is no natural beauty in the slum. No fruit trees growing, no plants and flowers, no pretty curtains or brightly decorated houses, no pictures or colours. There are just ramshackle homes that are mostly empty, save for a couple of possessions, and lots of mud.

"Beauty" is not a word that springs to mind when you enter the slum. Yet, if you choose to look deeper – to search beyond what can been seen with the natural eye into the unseen – you will find a depth of beauty hidden there that is so raw, resilient and real, it will take your breath away. It is not immediately obvious, but it is there all the same. Discovering it is life-changing and powerful. It is Gold.

Behind the TV images, government statistics and Oxfam adverts are the hearts and lives of real people. Men, women and children who, just like you and I, were knitted together in their mother's womb. Whom He created, fearfully and wonderfully, and whose lives are packed full of undiscovered potential and destiny.

They also need to hear the news that they have a Creator who deeply loves them, who has a plan and a purpose for their lives that is good. They need to be told that there is hope, redemption and love, right there, waiting for them.

They may not be able to see it, understand it, or even conceive of it, but nevertheless it is there.

The heart of their Heavenly Father longs for them to know this truth, to experience this reality, to be set free from every fear and bondage that lays claim to their lives.

So, just as we have so freely received this for ourselves, so now freely we must go and give it away.

It doesn't really matter where you live, or who are the "poor" that surround you. I say to my team all the time that *poverty wears many different faces and carries many different disguises.*

Mother Teresa said,

> *Being unwanted, unloved, uncared for, forgotten by everybody, I think that is a much greater hunger, a much greater poverty than the person who has nothing to eat.*

Whether you live in a slum or a palace, the inner city or the leafy suburbs, is irrelevant – that's just geography. What matters is what you are doing with what you have received; how you give of yourself each day, to demonstrate a life of hope, love and peace to those around you.

Glorious grace and limitless love

Whenever I walk the slums, I am challenged to lay down my judgment and pick up His mercy. To let go of my criticism and take hold of His acceptance. To leave behind my own ideals and expectations and lay hold of His grace, once again.

You and I are no more deserving of the transformational grace and love of Jesus than any slum dweller. We are not made worthy, righteous or deserving by what we have or haven't done, solely by what Jesus Himself did.

It is not our right to judge those around us. Instead it's our job to show mercy, love and grace to all people, in all circumstances, just as we ourselves have received it.

> *God saved you by his grace when you believed. And you can't take credit for this; it is a gift from God.* (Ephesians 2:8)

I have to admit that, at times, I have found the outrageousness of this grace offensive to my small, naturally limited mind.

However, I am learning to allow it to offend me. I want it to challenge and change my heart to become more like Jesus. At times I have failed to understand how it can be possible for this grace to cover not only the desperate situations I have come across, but also my own brokenness, mistakes and regrets. But still it does…

This grace confounds the wise. It challenges the religious. It shatters our man-made ideals and brings down the lofty. It is poured out in ways our human minds cannot always accept or understand. The fruit of it is beautiful and real. Its fragrance fills and overwhelms your senses. Once you collide with it, nothing is ever the same again.

God's heart for the poor is obvious – it is written about all through Scripture. His heart for the orphan and the widow is undeniable. He sees beyond the dirt, the addiction, the violence and bad choices. He sees beyond the mistakes, the anger and the regret. He sees those He loves, those He created, those He longs to call his own. He sees the Gold.

Whatever your political views on the issues of poverty in Africa, or of the situations around the world mentioned earlier, the Bible is clear that we cannot simply put our heads in the sand, pretend the poor are not there and ignore them. We can't hope that they will just go away or convince ourselves that it is someone else's responsibility to fight for justice, speak up for peace, and carry hope, love and righteousness to the hurting.

We have to be a part of the answer to these huge challenges – to be the hands and feet of Jesus to a hurting, broken, confused and frightened world.

Fashion accessories

About a year ago, on a beautiful Friday morning, I was driving into the pretty English countryside to spend the day at a retreat. Summer festival season was approaching, and I had many sermons I needed to prepare, so this would give me the time and space to do so.

As I drove, I was singing my favourite worship song and wondering what theme I should build my talks around when suddenly Jesus spoke to me. His voice came so clear and loud that I literally jumped. It was as if He was sat right there in the passenger seat. He told me,

"Nicola, tell the church that the poor are not a fashion accessory they get to wear around their necks."

I was stunned and also a little confused. I began to shake, so I quickly pulled the car over to the side of the road and turned the engine off.

"Jesus," I said, "I need you to say that again."

He spoke a second time:

"Nicola, tell the church that the poor are not a fashion accessory they get to wear around their necks."

I had never heard the Lord say anything like this before and to be honest I didn't really understand what He meant. However, I knew I had better quickly find out.

"Lord, I don't understand? Can you explain to me what you mean?"

He spoke to me about the trends we have in our churches. We often pursue fashions – maybe in our current style of worship, in the way we run our meetings, or in our pursuit of cultural relevance. We look at ministries who do things in a certain way that seems to bring success, and we decide *that must be the right way to do it.*

So, we begin to imitate them, but before long we realize that it's not working for us like it did for them, so we turn our attention to someone else who is doing it a different way. Suddenly, that becomes the latest thing to do.

It might be anything from the way in which we preach and teach, to how we handle prophetic ministry, to the kind of buildings we want to build, right down to the type of coffee we want to serve in those buildings. We hear about the latest "sexy" social action project that everyone is talking about and decide that we too will get in on the action … until that eventually falls out of favour and the next thing happens, and so on.

I saw what Jesus was saying. In our churches we have been guilty of wearing these things like fashion accessories – in one year and out the next. He said to me,

"Tell the church, 'Don't you ever treat the poor like that.'"

The poor are not a fashion accessory we get to wear to around our necks, in one year and out the next.

They are not there so that we can place a tick in our "mission" box and feel good about ourselves.

The poor, broken, marginalized, orphaned and widowed are at the centre of Jesus' heart. Those broken places that most of us fear and that if we are honest, we refuse to go to – Jesus runs straight into them and makes His home there. He pours out His love without restraint. We are called to go and do the same – to be His hands and feet and go mining for Gold.

Will this cost you?

Yes, absolutely!

In fact, it might cost you everything, but I can promise you that it will be worth it.

Lord, make me an instrument of your peace.
Where there is hatred, let me sow love;
where there is injury, pardon;
where there is doubt, faith;
where there is despair, hope;
where there is darkness, light;
and where there is sadness, joy.

O Divine Master, grant that I may not so much seek
to be consoled as to console;
to be understood as to understand;
to be loved as to love.

For it is in giving that we receive;
it is in pardoning that we are pardoned;
and it is in dying that we are born to eternal life.
St Francis of Assisi

7. Orphan-hood to Royalty

"When we begin to truly live out of the reality of Galatians 2:20 – It is no longer I that live but Christ who lives in me –Things begin to happen."

Gold carrier

The story of Esther is a familiar one to many and important enough in Scripture to warrant its own book. To me, there is no better example of a person being plucked from obscurity, thrust into a position of influence and dramatically used by God to bring about justice and mercy. Esther was a Gold-carrier. She just needed mentoring and steering in the right direction.

At the time the story was written, King Xerxes was in power. He was a highly successful and powerful ruler. One day he decided to throw a massive party for all of his nobles, officials and military leaders. This was going to be the party to end all parties!

It was extravagant, it was luxurious, and it lasted for one hundred and eighty days. Anyone who was anyone was there to enjoy it.

As the party was coming to an end, the king decided to throw a lavish banquet. This feast was to last an additional seven days and would take place in the grounds of his palace.

Everywhere was elaborately decorated with fine linens, marble columns, couches made of silver and gold, pavements lined with precious stones, gold chalices and an endless supply of wine. The guests were allowed to drink as much as they wanted and waiters were constantly positioned ready to fill their cups!

As the last day of the banquet arrived, the king called for Queen Vashti to be brought to him, dressed in all her splendour and beauty, wearing her royal crown. She was known to be extremely beautiful and he wanted to show her off.

However, Queen Vashti refused to come. This was scandalous!

Her disregard for both the king's request and his authority caused him to burn with anger. He consulted with his royal counsellors and advisors, asking for their wisdom in how to respond. Everyone was outraged and a decision was made.

The king issued a royal decree, stating that never again would the queen be allowed to enter the king's presence. Her royal position was taken away and she was effectively divorced.

After a while, when the king had calmed down, he set his mind to finding himself a new queen. Enter Esther!

Esther was an orphan girl who had been adopted by Mordecai (who was either her uncle or cousin). When Mordecai heard about the king's plan to find a new queen, he decided to send

Esther to the palace to take part in what was essentially a long, drawn-out beauty contest – the winner of which would get to be crowned queen.

Esther moved into the palace and entered into the long, complex regime of preparation for the day when she would eventually meet the king and, hopefully, astound him and win his heart. At this point, Esther has absolutely no idea of how the journey she had begun would unfold.

In due course, however, she won the king's approval and the royal crown was placed on her head. She was pronounced Queen Esther. This young orphan girl had been elevated to a position of royalty.

Maybe, like most of us would, at this point Esther had one of those, "Ahhhhh! I can't do this!" moments. In other words, "Who am I and what am I doing here? This is so far out of my comfort zone!" But this was just the beginning of the story. In due course she would risk everything to see God's purpose for her life fulfilled.

Sometime later, Mordecai fell out of favour with Haman, one of King Xerxes' highest-ranking officials, because he would not bow to him, refusing to worship anyone other than God. This incensed Haman, and the vengeful official decided to vent his fury not only on Mordecai, but on all the Jews in Xerxes' kingdom. Haman persuaded the king to give the order for every Jew – man, woman and child – to be massacred. Suddenly, all of God's people were under threat.

Things would have been very bleak for the Jewish people if not for Esther. God had raised her up for this purpose. Her position of royalty gave her direct access to the king. Here was a young Jewish girl with the opportunity to divert disaster and save a nation.

Esther sought an audience with the king, but she was taking a very big risk in attempting to influence him. How could such a serious decree be reversed without the king looking indecisive, foolish or weak?

Yet, God supplied Esther with the wisdom she needed in that moment, guiding her words so that she could make an irrefutable case. The king was persuaded and the course of history was changed. A whole nation of Jews was saved from a horrendous act of genocide.

One young orphan girl, raised into a position of royalty, with direct access to the king … and the results were amazing!

In the presence of the King

What does Esther's story mean for us today? What can it teach us about our search for Gold and our identity in Christ? Let me explain with another story.

One of my favourite scriptures is Hebrews 4:16 (NLT):

So let us come boldly to the throne of our gracious God. There we will receive his mercy, and we will find grace to help us when we need it most.

This scripture blows my mind. How is it possible that this mighty, majestic, universe-creating God, who wraps Himself in light as a garment and stretches out the heavens like a tent, who makes the clouds His chariot and set the earth on its foundations, says that you and I can walk right into His presence and simply ask Him for what we need?

I remember the day the truth of this scripture really dropped into my heart.

I had just left my three-year-old daughter at nursery school for the morning and I was walking back to my car. She had been having a tricky time transitioning to school life and it was not a rare occurrence for me to receive a phone call from her teacher, informing me of the "incident" of the day.

We had adopted her a year before and it had been a big adjustment for us all. She was boundless with energy, full of fun and packed full of cheekiness. She was quickly becoming both our greatest challenge and our deepest joy. However, things were not always easy for her. She had already had to navigate more difficult circumstances and situations in three short years than most of us do in a lifetime. Whenever I took a few moments to reflect on all she had survived, my heart would both burst with love and break with sadness at the same time.

I was so in love with my little girl and I longed for her to know what it was like to walk in freedom from the pain of the past that haunted her; to know a lightness of spirit, a safety in her soul, and the strength of the deep knowledge that she was loved.

As I was walking along the street, at the end of what had been a harder than normal week, my heart felt so heavy and I began to pray. However, I didn't get very far.

As soon as the word "Father" left my mouth, I was caught up in a vision.

I saw the Father. He sat on a throne in front of me and was looking straight at me with a smile on His face. There was a depth of compassion in His eyes that I had never experienced before. He leaned towards me and asked softly,

"What is it that you need sweetheart?"

As quickly as the vision began, it was over. I stood there in the street with tears streaming down my face. At this moment I realized that the scripture in Hebrews wasn't just a nice bit of poetry to display on our wall, or make into a cross-stitch to give to Grandma! It was a real, game-changing, stunning truth. It was true that the God of the universe had invited me to boldly approach His throne at any time, day or night – and that I could make my request and it would be heard.

Do you realize that you have access to Father God? Like Esther, you have been called into the presence of the King, and He is ready and willing to hear your request.

Orphan-hood to royalty

The incredible truth is that, just like Esther, you and I have been rescued from being an orphan and elevated to a position of royalty, with all of its privileges. We have become children of God, sons and daughters of the King. This means we now have access to the King of all Kings, the God of the universe.

Just think about that for a moment.

Think about the potential.

If God could use a young orphan woman to avert a national genocide, what could He do with you or me?

Because it gets much better than that. We don't just have access to the King, like Esther did. We have much more.

After Jesus was raised from the dead and appeared to His disciples, He made this shocking statement in Matthew 28:18-20:

> *All authority in heaven and on earth has been given to me. Therefore go and make disciples of all nations, baptizing them in the name of the Father and of the Son and of the Holy Spirit, and teaching them to obey everything I have commanded you. And surely I am with you always, to the very end of the age.*

In other words, Jesus tells us that all authority – in both the seen and unseen realms – belongs to Him and He chooses to give it to us. "Now take that authority," He tells us, "and use it to make disciples of all nations. Heal the sick, raise the dead and cast out demons. Go and do all the things I did and more besides!"

You and I don't just have access to the King – we carry the authority, presence and power of the King inside us.

Stunning!

I used to do this little activation exercise with my teams in Africa each morning, before they headed out into the slum communities for the day. I would ask them to hold out their hands in front of them and look at them for a while. Then I would say,

Look at YOUR hands. YOUR hands, not my hands...
YOUR hands carry authority and power – His authority and power.
Now go and lay them on someone who is sick and see what happens.

Next, I would ask them to take a moment to look at their feet, then I would say,

Look at YOUR feet. YOUR feet, not my feet...
YOUR feet carry authority and power – His authority and power.
Now go and find some darkness and walk straight into it and see what happens.

Lastly, I would ask them to place their hands over their mouths. Then I would say,

Feel YOUR mouth. YOUR mouth, not my mouth...
Your voice carries authority and power – His authority and power.
Now go and speak God's Word to someone and see what happens.

You see, when we begin to truly live out of the reality of Galatians 2:20 – *It is no longer I that live but Christ who lives in me* – things begin to happen.

When we allow Him to come and manifest Himself through us, through our everyday lives and our simple ways, something dynamic begins to happen.

Do not disregard the significance of your life! Do not disregard the power and potential of HIS life through YOUR life.

You were born to help change the world.

Whitechapel

I was walking around the East End of London recently in the Whitechapel district. We are in the process of opening our first UK missions base there. As I walked the Whitechapel Road, I painstakingly laid out to Jesus all the reasons why His idea of setting up a Dream Centre in this place was, in my humble opinion, utterly ridiculous.

I went into great detail, pointing out all the ways in which this was an impossible task for us (in case He wasn't already aware). We didn't have any money or resources and virtually no team. I had no idea how we could translate our experience of working with the urban poor in East Africa to British culture. I personally only had so many hours in a day to try and get a new base off the ground, while overseeing three national bases in East Africa, plus our international office.

I reminded Jesus of all these things and more. Like Esther, I was definitely having an "Ahhhhh! I don't know how to do this!" moment.

I felt overwhelmed, intimidated and utterly powerless in myself to make anything happen. Then He spoke and said this:

"Nicola, if you want to dwell in the realm of the miraculous, you have to learn how to live in the land of the impossible."

In other words, you won't see the miracles unless you first have need of them.

I want to suggest to you today that we are all called to live in the land of the impossible. In fact, I will go as far as to say that if we are not having, "Ahhhhh! Help me Jesus!" moments on a regular basis, we are not living the way He has called us to.

Why?

Because we were not born to live only in the land of the possible. We were born to live lives that intentionally, and on a regular basis, invade the impossible, infusing it with the endless possibilities of His love, power and life.

Your life is full of God-given potential.

Your life is full of God-given power.

Your life is full of God-given authority.

YOUR LIFE IS FULL OF GOLD

What are you going to do with it?

8. I See You

"Throughout history Jesus has constantly chosen to go to the weak, to those on the margins, with not much to recommend them ... to choose the ones that the rest of the world, and sadly sometimes the Church, disregards and labels as damaged … and says, 'I see you, I choose you. Come, follow me.'"

Those who know me well, will know that I started married life a very different person to the one I am today. Jesus has worked an incredible miracle in my life. He has taken a young girl of twenty-one years, who was crippled with insecurity, anxiety and self-doubt, and brought about an utter transformation.

If you had suggested to me all those years ago, that I would one day move my family to the other side of the world, to live on a continent I had never been to, and minister to some of the world's poorest and most broken … well, I would probably have laughed in your face and then promptly run away and thrown up!

When I married Simon, my childhood sweetheart, he was still a student at Bath University, which meant having to leave my home town, my family, all I'd ever known to move from London to live in the West Country. To be honest, it felt like the other side of the world, where people spoke with a funny accent and everyone seemed to drink cider!

This was huge deal for me. At this point of time, I couldn't have imagined anything bigger. Little did I know that thirteen years later I literally would be moving to live on the other side of the world.

So, there we were. I was shy, nervous and crippled with debilitating insecurity. Simon was studying Physics at university and was therefore a bit of a geek, as well as a major introvert. This was great news for me. I'd just arrived in a new city and knew no one there apart from Simon. It meant that we hardly had any friends and never really got invited anywhere – and for that I was deeply grateful!

I hated meeting new people. The thought of having to make polite conversation with someone I barely knew was terrifying. The idea of having to do so whilst trapped at a table at someone's fancy dinner party was even worse.

The one place we did go to every week was our church, which met in a beautiful old 1930's cinema in the city centre. The auditorium was huge, and the congregation was pretty large too. These two things combined meant that it was pretty easy for us to sneak in each Sunday morning and hide.

That was until one day we met a couple who changed our lives.

One Sunday morning we had crept into the back of church as usual and found "our seats" located at the side of the room. The meeting ran as normal and as everything was drawing to a close, we were gathering up our things to make a swift exit. We were then intercepted by the Pastor of the church making his way towards us.

To be completely honest with you, I did see him coming, but he walked towards us so quickly that my "run away as fast as you can" instinct wasn't quite fast enough. Suddenly there we were, face to face and trapped.

He gave us both a hug and shared an idea he'd had about running a new course for "emerging leaders". He thought we would be perfect candidates. I thought he had lost his mind!

We promised him we would "pray about it" and get back to him. In the spirit of being totally honest, I had zero intention of actually doing so. My plan was to send a quick email a few days later with a message along the lines of, "Thank you so much for your kind invitation, but our diaries are just too busy right now…".

Jesus, however, had a different plan.

To cut a long story short, we ended up doing the course. It was both the worst (most terrifying) and the best (most freeing) thing I had ever done. It stretched me at times beyond what I thought I could handle, but somehow, I managed to make it to the end. Out of it grew some beautiful, life-shaping friendships.

One of those was with a particular couple who, looking back, literally poured themselves out at great personal cost to continue to disciple Simon and I. They committed themselves to calling out the Gold in us – potential we were completely unaware of – long after the course had finished. They set us on a path of love, leadership and mission that would forever change our lives.

It's a powerful thing when someone truly believes in you and sees the potential of your life – especially when you don't see it yourself. Even more so when they are bold enough to call it out, then commit to walking alongside you, equipping you for the long term.

That is just what these people did. They opened their home to us and made us part of their family. They fed us, laughed with us and cried with us. They called out the Gold and prayed out the rubbish. They were the first people we told when we got pregnant and they were the first visitors, outside of our families, when our son was born. They taught us about marriage and parenthood.

They trained us in prayer and modelled to us what worship really was. They took us with them when they went out to speak and minister and constantly pushed us outside of our spiritual comfort zones. If there was a challenge to be brought, they brought it, and if there was need for a hug and some TLC, they brought that too.

Before then I had never had anyone in my life so tenaciously committed to seeing me fulfil my God-given calling. It changed our lives.

Looking back, we owe a huge amount of what we have done to that beautiful couple and their love and endless encouragement. I thank Jesus for the way that He placed us in their hearts. It really could only have been Jesus, as there was nothing in the natural to recommend us at all.

I was a broken, fear-based, mistrusting, insecure, uneducated young woman. My husband was a highly intelligent, independent, emotionally shut down introvert, who really had no need for conversation, or even people at times.

Well, that was how we would have described ourselves anyway. But when Jesus looked at us, He saw something totally different. Thankfully, so did this couple.

Throughout history Jesus has constantly chosen to go to the weak, to those on the margins, with not much to recommend them. He often seems to choose those that the rest of the world, and sadly sometimes the Church, disregards and labels as damaged. He reaches out to the uneducated fisherman and the woman with the questionable lifestyle, the crooked tax collector and the ones who twist His words for their own gain. To all of them He says,

"I see you, I choose you. Come, follow me."

He says the same to you and me.

Then He goes a step further and begins to breathe on the life-potential He has placed within us and something beautiful begins to form. Something powerful begins to take place. That which was once broken and disregarded starts to shine like Gold.

> *We can all draw close to him with the veil removed from our faces. And with no veil we all become like mirrors who brightly reflect the glory of the Lord Jesus. We are being transfigured into His very image as we move from one brighter level of glory to another. And this glorious transfiguration comes from the Lord, who is the Spirit.*
> (2 Corinthians 3:18 TPT)

Ambassadors

I will never forget the first time I met Mama N. We were about to start our first "Street Club" in a new community and a local church had given us permission to use their building. I say "building" but it was more like a tin shed, held together by bits of wood, propped up against metal sheets. Regardless, we were grateful to have somewhere to meet that had shade and we arrived there early to get everything organised.

We hadn't been there long when one of our staff members spotted two small children sitting under a nearby tree and went over to investigate. These two little ones were sat all alone. They were completely naked and their bellies were swollen up like balloons. They were clearly both too little and weak to be able to walk, so had been left under the shade of the tree to protect them from the intensity of the sun. They were each sat in a pool of their own diarrhoea and were so hungry they were busy licking it off the ground.

Their mama was nowhere to be seen.

Horrified by what she saw, our staff member sat down next to the two children and waited for their mama to return, which she did much later that afternoon.

Over the next few weeks we got to know Mama N and her situation more. She was twenty-three years old and had six children. Her youngest was born when she was only thirteen. Her husband was a brickmaker and would disappear for months at time, seeking work, trying to earn enough money to support his wife and children. They were incredibly poor, hungry, hopeless and alone.

Most days Mama N would leave her two youngest children under the tree and head off down to the main road to try and sell a small amount of maize, in order to raise some money to buy them food to eat. Some days she was successful, but most days she was not.

She was a woman of extremes. One day she would be almost wild with joy and excitement, the next lying on the floor of her tiny one-room house, unable to function, disconnected from her children and the world. I fell in love with Mama N the moment I met her, and my heart was broken for her family.

We began to visit her family as often as we could. We placed her children in a feeding programme and we helped secure free school places for those children who were old enough to attend.

We began to talk to her about Jesus and how He had a purpose for her life. We gave ourselves to speaking life and hope into her at every opportunity, encouraging her in the things she was good at and endeavouring to grow and support her in the things she was not. We called out the Gold from within her whenever possible.

I am very aware that we didn't always do things right. There were times that we intervened when, on reflection, we shouldn't have. Likewise, there were times when we should have intervened but, for one reason or another, didn't. We did one thing well though – we never gave up!

We visited Mama N come rain or shine. We were there when her two-year old was hit by a car. We held her hand and prayed with her when she discovered she was pregnant once again, and that baby number seven was going to make its entrance into the world regardless of whether she was able to feed and clothe it or not.

We went to family planning counselling with her (aiming to avoid a number eight!) and organised for a local pastor to support her and her husband in their marriage.

We secured her a free place in a class that taught spoken English for beginners and we arranged for training in varying trades and skills.

We cleaned her home when the family was too sick with typhoid and connected her with some Primary Health Care education to ensure that it didn't happen again.

We did all that we knew how to do to encourage, love and equip this beautiful chaotic unpredictable family.

And so the years went by … and we saw almost zero change!

I lost count of the number of times local villagers stopped us in the street to ask us why we bothered. Why didn't we just give up? Walk away? Find another family who would give us better results?

But we couldn't do that.

Jesus had brought this family into our lives and we had made a commitment to them. Jesus certainly hadn't given up on this family, so quite frankly neither would we. We were not in this relationship for what we would receive – we were in it for what we could give.

If we give of ourselves to love people for what we will receive in return, then I question if that love is genuine.

If we serve the poor in order to tick our missions box, then wear it as a badge of honour for all the world to see, I question whether our motives are pure.

We were not in relationship with Mama N for what we could get out if it ourselves. To be honest, if we were, we would have been no better than the men in the village who wanted to give her money in exchange for sex. We would have been guilty of non-sexual prostitution. We were not going to do that.

The bottom line is that we loved her. Scripture says that love is *patient* and *not self-seeking*, that love *always perseveres* and that it *never gives up*! (1 Corinthians 13).

Regardless of the lack of progress, the constant setbacks, the lies and the disappointments, we just kept on loving her. We would not give up our belief in her and the beautiful potential of her life.

Things moved forward, then they moved back again – a constant cycle over many years. However, slowly – very slowly – Mama N began to change.

I went to visit Mama N when I was in Uganda, just a few months ago. I was longing to see her as I had just received the news that she was now the proud owner of a small shop/stand at the side of the road that sold vegetables. This was so exciting!

As we arrived, both her and her children came running to greet us, with hugs and laughter all round. Mama N grabbed me by the hand and hurried me towards her little tiny shop. Her face was lit up with joy as she showed me the vegetables she had to sell and how beautifully she had displayed them for all to see. Her shop was made of wood. It was small and it leaned over to one side a bit, but it was hers! From its sales she was now able to pay the rent on her house and feed each of her children. This was the BEST day.

As we were chatting, something caught my eye. It was a tiny, torn, faded picture of me and her, pinned to the wall of her shop. I was surprised to see it and asked her what it was doing there.

In broken English she told me simply,

"I have your picture on my wall, so when my day is hard, I can look at you and remember that you are my friend. Thank you for always believing in me. Thank you for loving my family."

We sat outside her little shop for ages. We didn't actually talk much, she just held my hand and smiled, laughed, then smiled again. It was a moment of deep joy and, for me, one of great gratitude for the work God had done in her life. We sat there until evening began to draw in, then I went home and cried.

Mama N still has a long way to go, but I have so such hope for her! I believe in her completely. Growing up in a slum and being uneducated and poor does not define her. Only Jesus gets to do that, and He says that He loves her. He has plans for her to give her hope and a future, plans to prosper and to do her good (Jeremiah 29:11). We get the deep joy of coming into agreement with those truths over her life, then walking with her and seeing them unfold.

Sometimes all people need is for someone to believe in them. For someone to take the time to notice who they really are and speak truth, life and purpose into them.

I have been so blessed over the last 20 years to have always had one or two people who have consistently done this for me. To be honest, I don't know where I would be now without them. I am so thankful for them and to Jesus for placing me in their path.

We all need people to walk through the ever-changing seasons of life with – from the mountain tops to the valleys; people who are a tangible expression of God's love in our lives. Those who continue to believe in us, even when we don't believe in ourselves. Those who don't give up on us when we walk away; who encourage us to continue to dream, even in our darkest moments. Those who never surrender hope and continue to contend for us, championing our God-given destiny, regardless of the personal cost to them.

As Paul so eloquently writes:

> *But even if I am being poured out as a drink offering upon the sacrifice and service of your faith, I rejoice and share my joy with you all. (Philippians 2:17 NASB)*

This kind of discipleship takes commitment and time. It doesn't have to be complicated, but it does have to be consistent. It doesn't need to be extravagant, but it does need to be lived out. It doesn't need to eloquent, but it does need to be spoken.

One of our spiritual sons in Uganda recently wrote this:

"The Gospel is given sometimes in words, but it is usually louder in actions."

He's right. Words and actions are both powerful in themselves, but together they become unstoppable.

Who has God placed around you?

Who are the people you know that no one else has "seen"? The ones who desperately need someone to stop and say,

"Hey! I see you! I see the beautiful potential of your life. Let's discover more of it, in Jesus, together."

Who is the one waiting for you to call out the Gold in their life?

Who will you stand alongside and contend for – whatever the cost, however long it takes, never giving up?

For it is Christ's love that fuels our passion and motivates us, because we are absolutely convinced that he has given his life for all of us. This means all died with him, so that those who live should no longer live self-absorbed lives but lives that are poured out for him, the one who died for us and now lives again. So then, from now on, we have a new perspective that refuses to evaluate people merely by their outward appearances. For that's how we once viewed the Anointed One, but no longer do we see him with limited human insight.

Now, if anyone is enfolded into Christ, he has become an entirely new creation. All that is related to the old order has vanished. Behold, everything is fresh and new. And God has made all things new, and reconciled us to himself, and given us the ministry of reconciling others to God. In other words, it was through the Anointed One that God was shepherding the world, not even keeping records of their transgressions, and he has entrusted to us the ministry of opening the door of reconciliation to God. We are ambassadors of the Anointed One who carry

the message of Christ to the world, as though God were tenderly pleading with them directly through our lips.
(2 Corinthians 5:14–16 TPT)

9. The Simple Way

"My life is no longer about living to serve my own will and desires, its about the great joy of living to serve His … The world is in desperate need for God's people to stand up, be counted and pay the cost."

In this book we have looked at the two issues that have been stumbling blocks for humanity since the dawn of time – identity and ability. The age-old questions of *Who am I? What am I doing here? What is my purpose in life*?

Much confusion, frustration and pain results when we try to solve those questions in our own strength or copy the world's blueprint for "success". The answers are found only in Jesus as we discover both our God-given identity and God-given potential – the Gold within.

When our family first moved to live in Uganda in 2009, we were deeply challenged by the passage of scripture in James 1:27 that says:

Pure and genuine religion is the sight of God the Father is caring for the orphan and the widow in her distress and keeping oneself from being polluted by the world.

We decided we were going to very intentionally give ourselves to exploring this truth and learn more about the "pure and genuine" faith that James wrote about. How could we express that kind of faith in our daily lives?

We sought to strip away "religion" and replace it with love – simple, uncomplicated daily acts of love, both for and on behalf of Jesus. We sought to make this a huge part of our daily lifestyle of worship, learning how to declare with both our hearts and our hands who Jesus is and what He has done.

We painfully churned many questions over and over in our hearts and wept and prayed and spent many hours on our knees seeking answers. We challenged ourselves with questions like,

"Have we somehow over-complicated church?"

And,

"Have we spent too much time and energy on building the church ourselves, rather than following Jesus' command to "go and make disciples"?

> *Therefore go and make disciples of all nations, baptizing them in the name of the Father and of the Son and of the Holy Spirit, and teaching them to obey everything I have commanded you.*
> (Matthew 28:19 NIV)

And,

"Are allowing *Him* to build His church, how *He* wants to?"

And I tell you that you are Peter, and on this rock I will build my church, and the gates of Hades will not overcome it. (Matthew 16:18 NIV)

When we took the time to look back at how much time and money we had given to running the meetings of the church, compared to *actually living church* outside of its four walls, we were shocked and we were undone.

When we took stock of the money we had spent trying to improve our church buildings, while the poor were sick and dying from hunger, we had to ask ourselves the question,

Are we truly representing the Gospel? Are we really representing Jesus and His heart?

I don't claim to have all the answers to these questions and, to be honest, the more I pray about it the more questions I have. But one thing I am increasingly convinced of is this:

Surely the Gospel, surely church, surely having a relationship with Jesus, surely love should not be complicated.

Instead it should be simple and accessible to all.

Otherwise it would seem that the Gospel is just for the rich or the intellectual.

After two years of trying to unpack what we really believed about church, the Gospel, discipleship and love, while trying to discover afresh what "pure and genuine religion" was really about, we came up with something very simple. There really was nothing too mystical or complicated about it. This was it:

We would wake up every morning loving Jesus. We would spend time in His presence with a community of others who loved Him too, then we would just go…

It really was that simple: *we would just go.*

We would go into our local communities. We would go into the streets and alleyways of the slums and spend time with the people we met.

We sat in their homes, we ate together, we laughed, we cried, we shared our joys and our fears and we shared our faith.

It was very, very simple, but it seemed to work.

We didn't have anything to our credit that made us extra-special. We were not the most talented people, not the most charismatic. We didn't have a clever marketing strategy, huge amounts of money and an ultra-fancy website. We had virtually nothing! In the very beginning we had no money, no team, no profile, no brilliant ideas. It was scary and wonderful and, actually, very freeing.

All we had was love. What we carried was simply Jesus and a desire to see each and every person we met encounter that love and be equipped and released to live out their own God-given potential – to discover the Gold that God had placed within them.

Life in many parts of Africa is pretty basic. Poverty abounds and there are limited opportunities, a lack of education, not to mention a lack of basic utilities like clean water and electricity. Things that in the West, we take for granted.

But for all that, there is a simplicity to life there that I like. We soon discovered that in the midst of such simple living, simple things can make a huge impact.

We learned such a lot from this great continent about simplicity of life … and then God called us back to the UK!

Moving home

After living a reductive lifestyle and deliberately practicing a simple, uncomplicated expression of faith, we had to ask ourselves the question: *can this way of living work in the UK?*

If the Lord was calling us to a mission field in the East End of London, then I knew it had to – I just couldn't see it. In Uganda I had known how to carry the beautiful truth of Jesus, the power of simple love, expressed through my life. His love, using my hands though daily actions. His words on my lips to those all around me. How would that work now, in a new and (to me) strange culture?

I knew how to live out my faith in Africa, how to love my neighbours, make disciples and call out Gold in people's lives. It wasn't complicated or sensational – it was simple. How would that transfer to a country considered to be rich and well-educated, that appears to have everything it needs to survive? A place where time and friendship is so often overshadowed by the pursuit of material possessions. Could we make any kind of impact?

Of course, deep down I knew that Jesus is relevant to all people in all situations. Underneath the façade of abundance are still the issues of love and acceptance. The heart of every person in every nation of the world still resounds with the same basic questions:

"Do I have value? Am I loved?"

I also knew that the Western world needs Jesus just as much as Africa. But how were we to live out the "pure and genuine religion" James spoke of in a country that – although I was born and raised there – felt more alien to our family than Africa?

* * *

When we first arrived back in the UK and saw friends and family for the first time, the question we were most commonly asked was,

"How does it feel to be back home?"

This was not a straightforward question for us and we didn't really know how to answer it. For us, moving back to the UK was simply an act of obedience. We had no desire to do it. We only bought the plane tickets to the UK because the Lord told us clearly to do so – and we had spent many months prior to this trying our hardest to convince Him He was making a mistake.

Africa was not our "mission field" it was our home. The slum families we served were not our "projects" they were our friends. They were the ones we shared our hearts and our lives with. The ones we loved as deeply as if they were our own flesh and blood.

The idea of moving back to the UK was incomprehensible. It didn't feel like "going home" but "leaving home".

I remember the day we left Uganda. Our team gathered together in our compound to say goodbye and wave us off. It was such a lovely idea in theory, but in practice it was brutal on our hearts. As the bus pulled out of our gates and set off down the road, I desperately tried to look out of the dusty back window, to see those smiling faces one more time, waving and cheering us on our way. I felt like my heart was breaking and it took all of my inner strength and resolve not to scream at the bus driver to turn around and take us straight back home.

Yes, moving back to the UK was immeasurably harder than it ever was to leave. Trying to explain this to someone in the UK was met with the inevitable response,

"Well, why on earth did you decide to leave then?"

The answer is simple. Jesus asked us to. And if we don't respond to His call, then what is life all about?

The truth is this: as disciples of Jesus we don't own the rights to our lives anymore. We signed them over to Him the day we gave Him our lives. I belong to Him now and He owns me. I wouldn't want it any other way.

My life is no longer about living to serve my own will and desires, it's about the great joy of living to serve His.

God is good!

In Uganda we learnt this little song, which seemed to be sung in every place we ever went. It went something like this:

> "God is good, all the time
> and all the time, God is good
> And that's His nature."

This was quickly followed by a long, drawn out, loud and dramatically over-emphasized…

"WOW!'

…as each person looked at the others in the room and nodded in a deeply earnest and agreeable way!

My children always found that part highly amusing. Still today, if we are at church and the preacher declares that, "God is good" they will whisper a long, dramatic "Wowwww!" under their breaths, then try to contain fits of giggles.

It's not the most lyrically impressive song I've ever sung, but is nonetheless packed with truth.

I don't think I have ever questioned whether God is good. It's something I've always believed to be true. Regardless of what is happening around me, and what situations I find myself in – the good, bad or in-between – I know that God is good. This truth has never changed and it never will.

But I have learned that "being good" and "feeling good" are not the same thing.

The Bible makes it clear that there is a cost to becoming a disciple of Jesus. We only need to look at the life of Jesus Himself to discover how high that cost might be. Being His disciple means that we need to learn how to live out our lives based on how He lived His, seeking to follow His example and living by what He says.

Let's break that down a little more.

What does "following His example" mean for our lives?

Jesus was born, grew, learnt a trade and went to the temple.

He healed the sick, raised the dead and cast out demons.

He spent time with prostitutes, hung out with tax collectors, sought out those on the margins and made friends with the uneducated.

He upset the religious rulers and offended those in governmental power.

He was betrayed by one of those closest to Him, was accused of crimes He didn't commit, and was killed, choosing to lay down His life so that others might live.

Well, that's not a list for the faint hearted!

What about His teaching?

Jesus taught on many things, but His teaching included statements like this:

> *Whoever wants to be my disciple must deny themselves and take up their cross daily and follow me.* (Luke 9:23 NIV)

And,

> *Whoever tries to keep their life will lose it, and whoever loses their life will preserve it.* (Luke 17:33 NIV)

It's not a manifesto for those wanting a quiet, comfortable, risk-free life!

The truth is, discipleship is a call to sacrifice and surrender. Following Jesus is the call to selflessly lay down one's life, so that others might live. There is no associated guarantee that doing so will be easy. However, there is a beautiful promise that whatever is required, we can,

> *Come to me, all you who are weary and burdened, and I will give you rest. Take my yoke upon you and learn from me, for I am gentle and humble in heart, and you will find rest for your souls. For* ***my yoke is easy and my burden is light****.* (Matthew 11:28-30)

Yield

In Job chapter 22 we read,

> *Yield now and be at peace with Him;*
> *Thereby good will come to you.*
> *Please receive instruction from His mouth*
> *And establish His words in your heart.*
> *If you return to the Almighty, you will be restored;*
> *If you remove unrighteousness far from your tent,*
> *And place your gold in the dust,*
> *And the gold of Ophir among the stones of the brooks,*
> *Then the Almighty will be your gold*
> *And choice silver to you.*
> *For then you will delight in the Almighty*
> *And lift up your face to God.*
> *You will pray to Him, and He will hear you;*
> *And you will pay your vows.*
> *You will also decree a thing, and it will be established for you;*
> *And light will shine on your ways.*
> (Job 22:21-28)

These incredible verses show us clearly how we are to live. We are to "receive instruction from His mouth" and "establish His words" in our heart. In other words, pay attention to what He says then act on it!

We are to place our "gold in the dust" meaning to lay down everything outside of Him that has become precious to us.

Then, "the Almighty will be your gold and choice silver to you". He will become our Gold, our treasure, our everything.

Storing up treasure

My husband is obsessed with collecting wood. Not the pretty kind of wood that has some unusual markings or is all twisted up and delicate and beautiful – something we might enjoy looking at once it has been cleaned up and is displayed somewhere. Or, even better, put to some practical use in our home. No, he just likes ordinary bits of boring old wood!

Whenever there is a spare bit of wood hanging around, maybe from a tree we've had to trim back, or from an old fence panel that has fallen down in the wind, we absolutely, one hundred percent, without a shadow of a doubt cannot throw it away. We keep it all! It sits in our shed or gets put up in the loft and there it stays, unlikely to ever see the light of day again.

If I suggest that maybe we could burn it in our fire pit, or simply just put it in the car and take it to the dump, a slightly confused expression comes across Simon's face.

"But what if we need it one day?"

Between you and me that day has never come and I kind of doubt that it ever will!

It's fascinating, isn't it, the things we think we need in order to survive our everyday lives.

The world is constantly shouting at us, trying to dictate to us what those things are. Everywhere we turn, through various media, we are told that we'll have a happier life if we have a nicer wardrobe, a more secure home, a more attractive body, better relationships and a more exciting sex life.

It's easy, amidst this bombardment, to give in to the pursuit of comfort, enjoyment and self-fulfilment. But whilst these things aren't necessarily wrong in themselves, if they are all we're pursuing we will get nowhere. The life they offer is nothing more than an empty counterfeit.

In Philippians chapter three Paul writes,

> *But whatever were gains to me I now consider loss for the sake of Christ. What is more, I consider everything a loss because of the surpassing worth of knowing Christ Jesus my Lord, for whose sake I have lost all things. I consider them garbage, that I may gain Christ.* (Philippians 3:7-9)

We all spend our lives in pursuit of something. The question is not whether we will give up our lives, but *what will we give it up for?*

What is worthy of you spending your life on it?

Shipwrecks and beatings

Let's look at the life of Paul for a moment. He is a man of huge significance in the Bible. He was an amazing theologian who wrote at least thirteen (possibly fourteen) of the twenty-seven books in the New Testament. He was a brilliant teacher, a highly successful church planter, and on top of all that moved in healings, signs and wonders. The legacy of his life is immeasurable.

Yet, for all this, Paul was simply a man who knew what it meant to give his life to something that mattered. The incredible fruit of his life was produced at a heavy cost, but it was one he was willing to pay.

> *I have worked much harder for God, taken more beatings, and been dragged to more prisons than they. I've been flogged excessively, multiple times, even to the point of death.*
>
> *Five times I've received thirty-nine lashes from the Jewish leaders. Three times I experienced being beaten with rods. Once they stoned me. Three times I've been shipwrecked; for an entire night and a day I was adrift in the open sea. In my difficult travels I've faced many dangerous situations: perilous rivers, robbers, foreigners, and even my own people. I've survived deadly peril in the city, in the wilderness, with storms at sea, and with spies posing as believers. I've toiled to the point of exhaustion and gone through many sleepless nights. I've frequently been deprived of food and water, left hungry and shivering out in the cold, lacking proper clothing.*
>
> (2 Corinthians 24:23-28)

Again, not for the faint hearted.

What will be the cost for you and me to see individuals, families, or even whole communities transformed by the love of God? What will it cost to wholeheartedly love Jesus, love our neighbours, go and make disciples, and call out the Gold in their lives?

It probably won't involve beatings and shipwrecks.

It may instead look like deciding not to buy that bigger house in a nicer neighbourhood, instead choosing to live in the local council estate down the road, so that broken-down community can be transformed from the inside out.

It may look like choosing not to invest in that high interest savings plan to provide for a comfortable retirement, instead investing the money in a project to feed those who can't provide for themselves, or housing for those who have nowhere to live.

It may look like giving up your summer holiday abroad one year and instead taking all the single mums on benefits in your community away to the beach for a couple of days.

Or it may simply look like giving up your seat on the train for the woman who looks exhausted today.

I can't tell you what it will look like for you, but as Heidi Baker says, "Love looks like something."

Stand up!

The world is in desperate need for God's people to stand up, be counted and pay the cost.

You only have to turn on the news to see stories from around the world of sickness, disease, natural disasters, humanitarian crises, war, political manipulation, injustice and abuse.

If ever the world needed a message of HOPE, it is now.

If ever the world needed a message of PEACE, it is now.

If ever the world needed a message of LOVE, it is now.

It's time for the Church to stand up and be counted. To speak out for those whose voices have been silenced. To fight for justice for those who can't fight for themselves. To stand for righteousness in the midst of chaos and corruption. To call for peace in the middle of the threat of war.

We must be the generation who say, "No! There is a different way...

There is hope for that situation.

There is peace for that community.

There is a future for that people group.

There is healing for that broken nation.

There is Gold in that person.

There is Gold in that community.

There is Gold in that nation…

…and I will give my life to see it released, regardless of the cost.

It's time for the Church to wake herself up.

No longer can we sit on the side-lines, watching and praying from a distance. We have to get up and get involved. We have to be the answer, be part of the change. It's time to roll up our sleeves and actually get our hands dirty.

We need to stop being afraid and ruled by our instincts of self-preservation and protection.

We need to choose to be bold and courageous.

We need to stop excusing ourselves from getting involved.

We can no longer remain quiet about the things that matter and continue to play the game of political correctness.

We must make a stand for truth.

We have to cry out against injustice and speak up on behalf of the downtrodden.

We must be a voice for reconciliation and champions of hope.

We must care for the orphan and defend the rights of the widow.

Take up the challenge. Yield to Father God and allow Him to uncover the Gold in your life. Then go and spend your life in the pursuit of calling that Gold out of others. We have some challenging examples from Scripture, and there is a real cost to this. There is no cheap discipleship.

But it is simple.

You can share the love of God and be the hands and feet of Jesus daily, reaching out to touch those you encounter as you simply go.

Anything less would be a tragic waste of your Gold. So go. See what Jesus can do with the little you have, fully yielded to Him.

Our Story

In 2009 Simon and Nicola Neal followed God's call to Uganda. They packed up their home and their family and simply went to serve the poor. Shocked by the pain and suffering that they witnessed in the slums, they longed to see these communities discover God's love and potential for their lives. They got to know some of the families, started to pray with them and help in simple practical ways. That was the start of Revelation Life.

Since then, the NGO has grown. The team has increased and new bases have opened worldwide… we even grew into a new name: Every Life, which we feel, completely expresses our heart for people.

Today our team is made up of many passionate and committed people working in some of the most disadvantaged communities in Uganda, Kenya, Rwanda and the UK. With a motivation to share the love of God and working through discipleship in every area of life, we are seeking to empower communities to discover their potential in Jesus and to see people released in their gifts and callings, enabling them to become their own makers of change.

That's our story…..

Simon and Nicola are now based back in the UK, establishing an International Office from which to oversee the planting of further mission bases worldwide.

To find out more visit: https://everylife.org.uk